A World Built, Destroyed and Rebuilt

Rabbi Yehudah Amital's Confrontation
with the Memory of the Holocaust

By
Moshe Maya

Translated by
Kaeren Fish

KTAV PUBLISHING HOUSE, INC.
JERSEY CITY, NJ

YAACOV HERZOG COLLEGE
ALON SHEVUT, ISRAEL

2004

Copyright © 2005 Yaacov Herzog College

Library of Congress Cataloging-in-Publication Data

Maya, Moshe.
   ['Olam banui ve-harev u-vanui. English]
   A world built, destroyed, and rebuilt: Rabbi Yehudah Amital's confrontation
with the memory of the Holocaust / by Moshe Maya; translated by Kaeren Fish.
   p. cm.
   Includes "bibliographical abbreviations of works by Rabbi Yehudah Amital."
   Includes bibliographical references and indexes.
   ISBN 0-88125-864-4
   1. Holocaust (Jewish theology)   2. Amital, Yehudah – Views on the
Holocaust. 3. Religious Zionism.   I. Amital, Yehudah. Selections. English.
2004.   II. Title.
BM645.H6M37513 2004
296.3'1174 – dc22

2004018124

Cover design by Merav Rozen, tel. 972-2-673-7077
Typeset by Jerusalem Typesetting, www.jerusalemtype.com

Published by

KTAV Publishing House, Inc.
930 Newark Avenue
Jersey City, NJ 07306
orders@ktav.com
www.ktav.com
Tel. (201) 963-9524
Fax. (201) 963-0102

Yaacov Herzog Colleg
Alon Shevut 90433, Israel
Tvunot Press
Alon Shevut, Israel
office@etzion.org.il
www.herzog.ac.il
Tel. 972-2-993-7333 (Israel)
Tel. (212) 732-4874 (USA)
Fax. 972-2-993-2796

Contents

Preface

A CATACLYSM OF UNPRECEDENTED proportions in Jewish history, the Holocaust has shaped the identity of many contemporary Jews, affecting their religious, social and political attitudes. Yet some find it too overwhelming to face, and consequently force it out of their consciousness.

This volume distills the attempt of one prominent educator, himself a Holocaust survivor, to confront the memory of that watershed event. While the urgency of survival has prodded him to prodigious accomplishments, the nagging memory of the Holocaust has forced him to reassess some deeply-held convictions. Within his religious circle, his is a maverick approach, which he has maintained courageously in the face of no small amount of opposition. In order, then, to understand properly Rabbi Amital's response to the Holocaust, it is important first to locate his position within his cultural and religious milieu.

Religious Zionism and its Place within Orthodoxy

Since the nineteenth century, it has been customary to view Judaism as being divided into several religious denominations. Yet many Jews today, in the Diaspora and especially in Israel, regard their Jewish identity in purely cultural and national terms, with little or no religious content. Among those who do retain a religious element in their self-definition as Jews, only the Orthodox denomination maintains a sizable presence in Israel; however, this community is by no means monolithic. It is subdivided into a number of groups that differ in both ideology and lifestyle, among them Haredim of various stripes (Hasidic, "Lithuanian," and Sepharadic) and Religious Zionists. (They are also termed ultra-Orthodox and National-Religious, respectively.) Though all these groups adhere to the strictures of Jewish Law, the former advocate a more insular and anti-modernist religiosity, while the latter favor participation in the endeavors of general society, sensitivity to the flow of history and an activist posture.

A major point of disagreement concerns their respective attitudes towards the Zionist project and the State of Israel. The Haredim adopt a neutral or negative attitude towards the State, since it is dominated by secularists and does not follow Jewish Law. Religious Zionists, who emphasize both the religious and the national components of Jewish identity, not only hold a positive view of the State but ascribe to it religious, and sometimes messianic, significance. Many Haredim believe that Jewish sovereignty in the Land of Israel must follow the coming of the Messiah, while Religious Zionists reverse the order: the restoration of Jewish sovereignty will bring the Messiah, and, in fact, represents a stage in the redemptive process.

While this dispute may seem purely theoretical, it actually has many practical ramifications, none more pronounced and pained than the question of service in the Israel Defense Forces. In keeping with their views, the Haredim largely avoid military service (with a notable exception among Sepharadic Haredim). Religious Zionists, on the other hand, view army service as a matter of ethical and religious obligation. To this end, Religious Zionist leaders, among them Rabbi Amital, set up the "*hesder*" framework, a five-year program in which students divide their time between the service in the military and Torah study in a yeshivah, a religious academy.

The preeminent ideologue and inspiration of the Religious Zionist community in Israel is Rabbi Avraham Yitzhak ha-Kohen Kook (1865–1935), the first Ashkenazic Chief Rabbi of Mandatory

Palestine. A prolific writer, seminal thinker and charismatic leader, he felt that a national renaissance could be attained by harnessing both the religious and the nationalistic forces within Jewish existence. His influence spread after his death, largely through the efforts of his son, Rabbi Zvi Yehudah ha-Kohen Kook, and the latter's disciples.

Yet Rabbi Zvi Yehudah's interpretation of his father's thought was a very specific one, highlighting its messianic aspects. He saw the founding of the State as a miracle of the first order, and after Israel's astonishing victory in the Six Day War in 1967, when people had expected a second Holocaust to take place, many came around to his way of viewing contemporary reality. The Six Day War, and even more the crisis engendered by the Yom Kippur War in 1973, also propelled Rabbi Zvi Yehudah's followers to concrete action. They spearheaded the effort to settle Jews in the areas of the Land of Israel liberated in the Six Day War, specifically Judea, Samaria and Gaza. They attributed to this not just political significance, but primarily religious and redemptive significance: they would hasten the redemption by fulfilling the commandment to settle the land. For this reason, they have also been at the forefront of the opposition to ceding these territories, from Camp David to Oslo and beyond.

Rabbi Amital: A Brief Biography

Rabbi Yehudah Amital (Klein) was born in 1924 in Transylvania, Hungary. During the Second World War he was sent, along with a number of his friends, to a Nazi labor camp. Members of his own family as well as others of his community perished in the concentration camps. Upon his liberation, he made his way to Palestine, arriving during Hannukah 5705 (1944). Thereupon, he resumed his yeshivah studies at Yeshivat Hebron and received rabbinic ordination from Rabbi Isser Zalman Meltzer.

While in yeshivah, Rabbi Amital joined the "Haganah," the precursor of the Israel Defense Forces. During the Israeli War of Independence, he served in Battalion 79 and fought at Latrun and in the Galilee. After demobilization, he studied and taught in Pardes

Hannah, and then, together with his father-in-law, founded Yeshivat HaDarom in Rehovot. He also instituted a post-high-school teacher training program, which was a precursor of the *hesder* system.

A year after the liberation of Gush Etzion in the Six Day War, he was offered the position of *rosh yeshivah* of the newly-founded *hesder* yeshivah there, Yeshivat Har Etzion. Under his leadership, along with that of his colleague Rabbi Aharon Lichtenstein, it grew into the largest of the *hesder* yeshivahs. While this would seem to place him at the heart of the Religious Zionist consensus, his views have set him apart from the mainstream.

During the Lebanon War in 1982, Rabbi Amital went public with a new political and ideological position, moderating his views on territorial compromise and decrying overemphasis on settling the land at the expense of other religious values.[1] In 1988, he founded Meimad, which began as an ideological-educational movement and evolved into a political party. In 1996, in response to the murder of Prime Minister Yitzhak Rabin, he was invited to serve as a Minister in the Israeli government, in charge of religious-secular relations and Israel-Diaspora relations. After serving as a minister, Rabbi Amital returned to his full-time educational work as *rosh yeshivah*.

The Writing of this Volume

Rabbi Amital writes and speaks as an educator and rabbinic scholar, not as a professional philosopher. His treatments of the Holocaust and the religious significance of the State of Israel stem from deeply held beliefs and insights forged in the tumult of his inner religious life and his engagement with communal issues and with students' questions and struggles. He presents his ideas not in the measured tones of philosophical discourse, but rather in the traditional manner of exegesis of biblical and rabbinic texts, with an emphasis on the sources' living meaning for his listeners. His words contain not

---

1.   See Rabbi Y. Amital, "Political" and "Cry of an Infant" (all bibliographical references appear at the end of this volume).

just analysis, but also moral exhortation and the practical application of ideas to burning issues of the day.

Moshe Maya, the author of this study, is not a disciple of Rabbi Amital. His training is as a historian, and he initially approached this study as an attempt to discern a thinker's worldview from the kind of traditional discourse described above. As a response to real situations and to the actual needs of students and the community, this type of discourse is less systematic but more highly charged than standard philosophical thought. Amassing a wide range of Rabbi Amital's writings and statements, the author set out to examine their manner of presentation, use of sources, and changes over time. Only after studying the written record did he interview Rabbi Amital, thereby confirming his analysis of the latter's thought.

Yet, during his research, the author came to believe that Rabbi Amital had an important and rarely-heard message, and he wished to bring it to broader attention. We hope that this English version of his book will add an important voice to the broader dialogue on Holocaust theology. It is a voice that should be heard not only by Rabbi Amital's own Religious Zionist community, but also by other branches of Orthodoxy, other Jewish denominations, and other faith communities. We trust that something of Rabbi Amital's combination of wisdom and perspective, passion and commitment, and morality and humanity, will be communicated through these pages.

The publication of this English volume would not have been possible without the vision and enthusiastic commitment of Dr. Shmuel Wygoda, head of Yeshivat Har Etzion's affiliated Yaacov Herzog College, and Bernard Scharfstein, president of Ktav Publishing. Kaeren Fish skillfully translated the book, and Michael Platt assisted in the research and compiled the index. Our thanks to them all.

Reuven Ziegler, Editor
Yeshivat Har Etzion
Yom Ha-Shoah 5764

Introduction

THE HOLOCAUST has left an indelible impression upon Rabbi Yehudah Amital's world-view;[1] as he himself has expressed it, "I see the influence of the Holocaust in everything."[2] Rabbi Amital views the Holocaust as the most terrible catastrophe in all of Jewish history:

> There is something that is more terrible than the destruction of the Temple... if a person does not feel that the Book of Lamentations and the *Kinot* [of *Tishah be-*

1. Most of Rabbi Amital's publications were first presented as *sihot* (discourses) and transcribed by students, or were written to students during their periods of military service. They appeared within the publications of Yeshivat Har Etzion, including *Daf Kesher, Alon Shevut, Alon Shevut Bogrim* [all Hebrew] and *Alei Etzion* [English]. Even the *HaMa'alot MiMa'amakim* collection (Jerusalem and Alon Shevut 1974) contains mainly lectures delivered orally following the Yom Kippur War. A bibliography of Rabbi Amital's writings appeared in *Alon Shevut Bogrim* 3, 1994, pp. 103–110, and in *Alei Etzion* 2, 1995, pp. 65–74. Since then, dozens of further articles and lectures have been published, a number of which are available on Yeshivat Har Etzion's Virtual Beit Midrash, http://www.vbm-torah.org. A large portion of these were printed almost verbatim as delivered, and close to the time of their delivery, but some have been processed by students and other listeners and should therefore be approached with caution.

2. "Forty Years Later," p. 88. For the reader's convenience, the discourse is reprinted at the end of this volume.

Av] pale beside the Holocaust, then he is belittling the
Holocaust.[3]

The memory and pain of the Holocaust color the portrait of the
world thereafter: "The Holocaust has become deeply ingrained
within the consciousness of our people."[4] It is part of what being
Jewish means in our generation[5] and in future generations: "This
trauma will pursue the nation – despite all the mechanisms of denial – for generations to come."[6]

The religious sphere likewise must be reassessed in light of the
Holocaust. An example of such reassessment is to be found in Rabbi
Amital's treatment of the foundation of *avodat Hashem* (Divine ser-
vice) in our times:

> In *The Duties of the Heart*, Rabbenu Bahya ibn Pekuda
> develops the notion that our service of God is based on
> gratitude to Him. "The Gate of Unity" and "The Gate
> of Distinction" precede "The Gate of Divine Service."

3. "Confronting the Holocaust," p. 45. This discourse was delivered to the
Yeshivah in July 1998. For the reader's convenience, the discourse is reprinted
at the end of this volume. It should be noted that the Hassidic leader Rabbi
Kalonymus Kalman Shapira wrote on November 18, 1942 in the Warsaw
Ghetto: "Only until the end of 5702 [summer of 1942] was it the case that
such sufferings were experienced before. However, as for the monstrous tor-
ments, the terrible and freakish deaths of malevolent monstrous murderers
devised against us, the House of Israel, from the end of 5702 and on – according to my knowledge of rabbinic literature and Jewish history in gen-
eral, there has never been anything like them" (*The Holy Fire*, ed. N. Polen,
Northvale, NJ, 1994, p. 132–3). Compare Rabbi Hutner's lecture delivered on
April 12, 1976 (see bibliography). See also Eliach; Piekarz, pp. 349–353.
    This discussion touches on the issue of the uniqueness of the Holocaust.
See, for example, Fackenheim, "Faith," pp. 30–31; E. Schweid, "Was the
Holocaust 'Unprecedented?'" *Iyyun* 37, 1989, p. 271ff [Hebrew]; Y. Bauer,
"Is There an Explanation for the Holocaust?" *Yalkut Moreshet* 52, 1992, p. 123
onwards [Hebrew].
4. "Forty Years Later," p. 88.
5. "A World Built," p. 27.
6. "Nation Before Land," p. 12. See also *HaMa'alot MiMa'amakim*, p. 74.

In "The Gate of Distinction," Rabbeinu Bahya expands on the need to constantly think about God's kindness; the obligation of divine service thus springs from belief in His unity and recognition of His good. Rabbeinu Bahya addresses this at the opening of "The Gate of Divine Service" as well.

More than a few modern rabbis and preachers have continued to espouse the idea of gratitude as a basis for worshipping God. Such, for example, was Rabbi Dessler's approach, in the years preceding the Shoah.[7] The question is, understandably: after the awesome devastation of the Jewish People in the Holocaust, how – if at all – can we still talk about our worship of God being based on gratitude or recognition of God's grace?[8]

The way of Rabbeinu Bahya, which builds the service of God upon the foundation of gratitude, is no longer possible. In the wake of the Holocaust, thanks and praise for God's mercy towards His creation can no longer be the worshipper's starting point. Only by ignoring the Holocaust can we adopt such an approach. The readiness to re-examine the basis of our relationship with God assumes that this relationship must rest on profound truth, "and not on falsehood or fawning flattery."[9] It is difficult to find anywhere in Orthodox Judaism a statement comparable to this assertion that the Holocaust has blocked a certain path of man's Divine service.

Rabbi Amital proposes a different foundation: a way based on the love of God, in the sense of the declaration that "Even if He kills me, I will still trust in Him" (Job 13:15). This is the desperate

7. Dessler, *Strive*, vol. 1, p. 153–5.
8. "Confronting the Holocaust," p. 48.
9. Ibid., p. 49. An approach that seeks to confront evil with no attempt to cover it up is to be found in the words of the Sages: "These prophets knew that their God is truthful, therefore they would not [hypocritically] flatter Him" (Jerusalem Talmud, *Berakhot* 7:3; *Megillah* 3:7; compare Babylonian Talmud, *Yoma* 69b). See also "Confronting the Holocaust," pp. 48–50.

search of one who has found alternate paths closed before him. In this context, Rabbi Amital quotes the words of Rabbeinu Bahya:

> If You incinerate me in flame, I will continue only to love You and rejoice in You. It is as Job (13:15) said, "Even if He kills me, I will still trust in Him" ... Our sages said (*Shabbat* 88b), by way of derivation, "Though He constricts and embitters me, 'He will sleep between my breasts' (Song of Songs 1:13)."[10]

This is a search conducted with a profound sense of God's presence; there is not even the slightest hint of a claim here that God is absent, or even that He is "hiding His face" (*hester panim*).[11]

The shock of the Holocaust is threatening to a religious outlook predicated on God's immanence, wherein God sees everything and is involved in the world's fate.[12] There are those who maintain that the shock of the Holocaust caused a deep fracture in the world, following which "everything is undermined."[13] Others maintain that despite the shock, the Holocaust did not bring about a turning point in religious thought, and that it can be explained and its significance understood within the framework of the traditional

---

10. Rabbeinu Bahya, *Duties of the Heart*, Gate of the Love of God, chapter 1.
11. The claim that God "hides His face" is to be found in many of the modern theological responses to the Holocaust. The sense of Divine presence that arises from Rabbi Amital's words here cannot accept such a claim. I shall discuss this subject at length below.
12. The influence of the Holocaust on Jewish faith and religious thought has been the subject of extensive study and discussion. See, for example, D. Michman's list of literature, "The Influence of the Holocaust on Religious Judaism," *Fundamental Changes in the Jewish Nation in the Wake of the Holocaust*, Jerusalem 1996, p. 613, note 1 [Hebrew], and elsewhere in the article; ibid., "Faith," esp. note 2.
13. "The Holocaust, too, challenges Jewish faith from within, but the negativism of its challenge is total, without light or relief. After the events associated with the name of Auschwitz, everything is shaken, nothing is safe" (Fackenheim, "Faith," p. 30).

religious modes of thought that had prevailed previously.[14] Several intermediate positions fall between these two stances.[15]

Rabbi Amital will neither accept nor propose any religious explanation for the Holocaust, nor will he attribute religious significance to it. At the same time, he will not banish the Holocaust from his service of God. He cannot and will not ignore it; it influences his views on religion and its limits, while his fundamental position remains a profound sense of Divine closeness.

As a yeshivah head and educator, Rabbi Amital is sensitive to changes in reality, and he is aware of the religious need for reevaluation of religious positions.[16] In this regard, he perceives himself as a disciple of Rabbi Avraham Yitzhak Kook.[17] The same applies to his understanding of the teachings of Rabbi Kook[18] himself. In a lecture on the significance of Rabbi Kook's teachings in our times,

14. For example, M. Verdiger, *The Holocaust as a Theological Turning Point*, Ramat Gan 1998 [Hebrew]. Verdiger concludes that the main trends of post-Holocaust religious thought show no evidence of a theological turning point, since the thinkers address the religious significance of the Holocaust within the conceptual framework of existing modes of religious thought; they do not break out of these boundaries.

15. E. Schweid, for example, describes "the theological thinking that grapples with historical events representing manifestations of evil that undermines faith in a just and beneficent Divine Providence" as thinking that "generally gives expression to a religious crisis whose start precedes those events;" "those faith-undermining events thus become amplified and accelerated manifestations of the religious crisis" (E. Schweid, "The Holocaust at the End of the Twentieth Century from a Theological and Scholarly Perspective," *Jewish Studies* 39, 1999, p. 35 [Hebrew]).

16. Rabbi Amital likewise addresses the need for halakhic reevaluation in light of the changing reality: "The Hazon Ish writes that for halakhic rulings one needs knowledge of Halakhah as well as an evaluation of reality… the law may be simple, but the evaluation of reality is complex" ("Not Everything," p. 97).

17. "But specifically because of what I learned from [Rabbi Kook's] teachings, I believe that we, the followers of his approach, must view the current situation in accordance with reality, and not quote passages written eighty years ago without considering their applicability to our period" ("Religious Significance," p. 142). I shall quote excerpts from this discourse below.

18. For the remainder of this volume, "Rabbi Kook" will refer to Rabbi Avraham

Rabbi Amital asked: "Is it at all possible to speak of the significance of things that were written at such a great qualitative distance?"[19] Any attempt to evaluate the significance of Rabbi Kook's teachings for our generation must be processed through the filter of the Holocaust, which no one foresaw at that time.

Rabbi Amital sits squarely within the Religious Zionist camp;[20] he emerges from this environment and addresses himself to it. This is true both on those occasions when he comes out in support of it, and on those when he opposes it. The Holocaust causes him to examine the positions that had previously prevailed in Religious Zionist circles. Often his words seem like a delayed reaction to the memory of the Holocaust, a reaction that has waited, ripened and awakened much later, in light of events that have taken place over the course of the years. Religious Zionist thought generally holds that God reveals Himself in historical processes and events; His direct actions in history leave signs that may be revealed and identified, and His general intention may be established through interpretation and understanding of events. In this area, Rabbi Amital has been one of the leading lights of Religious Zionism. However, over the course of the years, the memory of the Holocaust has come to influence Rabbi Amital's perception of this issue.

One of the subjects we shall examine is the theological explanation of the relationship between the establishment of the State of

Yitzhak ha-Kohen (RAYH) Kook; so as to avoid confusion, his son will always be referred to by his full name, Rabbi Zvi Yehudah ha-Kohen (RZYH) Kook, or Rabbi Zvi Yehudah.

19. "Ethical Foundations," p. 14. I shall return to this subject below.
20. The scope of the present work does not allow for a comprehensive definition of the ideological, theological or sociological aspects of "Religious Zionism," a list of its guiding personalities or a review of their respective positions with regard to the subjects under discussion. An attempt at an ideological and theological demarcation of Religious Zionism was recently undertaken by Schwartz in several volumes: *Faith*; *Land*; *Religious Zionism*; and *Challenge*. In his article, "Paths in the Study of Religious Zionist Thought," in N. Ilan (ed.), *A Good Eye: Dialogue and Debate in Jewish Culture*, Tel Aviv 1999, p. 564 ff [Hebrew], Schwartz addresses some of the debate sparked by his works.

Israel and the Holocaust. Together with praise and thanks to God for the establishment of the State, Rabbi Amital has been careful to reject – over and over, relentlessly – any theological connection between this event and the Holocaust. Any such connection is regarded in his eyes as *hillul ha-Shem* – a desecration of God's Name. In this regard, his stance is radically different from that of many other Religious Zionist leaders, the great majority of whom perceive a causal connection – either theological, historical or both – between the two phenomena.

The memory of the Holocaust stands at the foundation of Rabbi Amital's moral positions. In this sphere, its effect on him is explicit and conscious. Here, too, he sets himself apart from many other Religious Zionist rabbis and educators.

* * *

Most of what Rabbi Amital has said has been presented in the context of his position as a *rosh yeshivah* and educator responding to the needs of his students. The teachings of an educator are an "oral law," and depend on speech, silence, tones and facial expressions.[21] His is not a philosophical-theological doctrine, which must relate to other analytic approaches, both internal and external. Rather, it prefers to relate in a concrete fashion to the subject under discussion, and to provide a religious, human and educational response to the needs of the community and the students. The need to respond to concrete problems takes precedence over careful preservation of philosophical coherence. His statements – both in form and in content – are

21. See Rabbi Amital's comments in the introduction to *HaMa'alot MiMa'amakim*. From this point of view, Rabbi Amital is one of those educators whose teaching is an "oral law" and whose writings are a de-facto concession. An educational statement or action that is intuitive by nature is often identified and formulated only "after the fact." Writing about pedagogic subjects can become a written commentary on a pedagogic action or statement, without any organized pedagogic method preceding it. See, for example, Y. Perliss, "A Jewish Man from Poland," *Ghetto Fighters* 1986, pp. 46–47 [Hebrew]; Z. Kurzweil, *The Pedagogic Teachings of Janusz Korczak*, Tel Aviv 1968, p. 108 [Hebrew].

formulated in the traditional formulations of Jewish culture: as discourses of the *rosh yeshivah*, as sermons, ethical exhortations, citation and exegesis of biblical verses, and halakhic guidance.

Rabbi Amital's words were not spoken or written during the Holocaust years, and they do not carry – chronologically – the primary and formative weight of what was said or written at that time.[22] At the same time, his reaction is an authentic religious one, both in its classical religious-Jewish form and in another sense as well: it lacks the complacency of a perspective formed at a distance in time. It touches a real essence, from within which the questions are posed. It contains something of what E. Schweid says of thinkers who lived under the Nazi occupation:

> It may be claimed that uniquely only they could contain the directness of empathetic insight into human experience, behavior and inner response under extremely abnormal situations…. [T]hese thinkers could achieve a clarity unrivaled by others who, though possessing a tranquil mind and historical perspective, lacked the ability to touch that extraordinary reality from with so as to be able to ask the right questions, or did not experience the hidden spiritual power out of which one can adequately answer such questions.[23]

22. E. Schweid (*Wrestling*, p. xiii ff) draws a distinction between philosophical study of religious questions and the initial religious human experience, which reflects a "realm of tangled feelings of suffering, mourning and guilt" (ibid. p. xxii). As a first step towards philosophical study that deals with "problems of religion and humanism – theological, ethical, political – and the existential situations raised by modernity" (ibid. p. xv), Schweid proposes a return to the theoretical literature that was created under the Nazi regime during the Holocaust, and to extract its conceptual content. The understanding that is to be gained from this religious challenge may show the way for those seeking a philosophical investigation.

23. Ibid., pp. xviii. Schweid writes further: "…[O]nly a few rare individuals achieved such insights and felt an absolute need to express themselves, their feeling of necessity being itself an overpowering insight which sprang forth as a religious revelation from an unfathomed depth…" (ibid.).

Chapter one

"Whoever Among You Remains:" The Ramifications of Survival

LIKE ANY EDUCATOR, Rabbi Amital carries his life experience into his teaching.[1] As the head of a *hesder* yeshivah and someone who has been a leading figure in Religious Zionism for decades, he presents and explains to his students the Jewish and Israeli experience and the history of the nation and State of Israel during the past half-century. Moreover, Rabbi Amital speaks as a Holocaust survivor. This perspective is part of his educational and spiritual message.

I. NAME

The name a person chooses for himself indicates the identity he assumes. Rabbi Amital changed his name from "Klein" to "Amital." "The new name, meant to remind him that he was a coal plucked from the fire, was inspired by a verse in the Book of the prophet Micah,"[2] namely, "And the remnant of Jacob shall be among many

---

1. See Y. Elitzur and A. Shama, "With the Return of the Journal," *Alon Shevut* III, 1985, pp. 1–2.
2. M. Rahat, *Ma'ariv Weekend Supplement* July 22, 1988, p. 6 [Hebrew]. See also A. Milner, "The Fourth Way," *Ha'aretz Supplement* December 15, 1995, p. 30, column 4 [Hebrew]. The name "Amital" was a pen-name from the period of the War of Independence, which was later retained as a family name.

peoples like dew from God, like the showers upon the grass that does not wait for any man nor place its hope in mortals" (5:6). In other words, the "remnant of Jacob" (*ami* – i.e., "my nation") is like dew (*tal*). The medieval exegete Rabbi David Kimhi (Radak) comments:

> "And the remnant... shall be" – i.e., those who shall remain after being purified (by fire), as it is taught (Zachariah 13:9): "And I shall bring a third of them through the fire and I shall refine them as silver is refined, and I shall try them as gold is tried; He shall call out My name and I shall answer him; I shall say 'He is My nation' and he shall say 'The Lord is my God.'"[3]

The following verse is no less meaningful and relevant: "And the remnant of Jacob shall be amidst the nations, among many peoples, like a lion among the animals of the forest, like a young lion among the flocks of sheep, who – if he passes through – tramples and tears in pieces, with none to deliver" (5:7).[4] These verses are full of significance for someone who interprets reality in accordance with the hints provided in the verses of the Bible, and imbues reality with

---

3. Radak continues: "'Among many peoples...' – and Israel shall be among them like dew from God, for dew comes from God from the heavens, and someone who awaits it does not await a person who shall bring it, but rather awaits only God, for it is He who brings dew and rain to the earth. Likewise, Israel place their hope for that salvation in no one but the blessed God, for it is He who saves them and there is no savior but Him. For they shall be a small nation and the nations that gather against them shall be many, and who but He can save them? And His salvation will descend to them like dew falling from the heaven."

4. Another verse from the Book of Micah provides one of the key themes in Rabbi Amital's eulogy for his students who fell in the Yom Kippur War. Twice he repeats the expression taken from verse 4, "eight princes of men." This verse provides the name and central motif of the memorial booklet published by the Yeshivah: *Eight Princes of Men*, Alon Shevut, 1975.

Biblical meaning.[5] A person who interprets the words of the prophets as applying within his own reality, and gives the prophetic verses concrete significance, understands the description of the "remnant of Israel" and the interpretation of Radak that speaks of "a third of Israel" as referring to a specific situation in the future. The sense of aloneness and alienation "among many peoples," with "all the world on one side and we on the other side" – a feeling mentioned more than once by Rabbi Amital – arises in this chapter that speaks of the "remnant of Jacob" being located among many peoples, but not looking to any mortals for help.

2. THE SURVIVORS' MISSION

The fact of having been saved from a place where millions perished troubled Rabbi Amital for many years; it has been a formative experience, whose impression is noticeable in much of what he has said, written and done. He understands salvation as indicating selection, which in turn indicates a mission and a responsibility,[6] even if he is plagued at times with doubts as to the actual nature and purpose of this mission. He testifies as follows:

> During the past forty years, I have often recalled the horrors that I lived through. Millions of Jews were murdered in the Holocaust – yet I was saved. Was I saved because God singled me out and made sure that I would not suffer the same fate as millions of others of our people? Or rather was it a mere case of chance? The verse states, "And I will surely hide My face on that day" (Deut. 31:18). When God hides His countenance from us, it is because, as the verse tells us, "And if you

5. See, for example, *HaMa'alot MiMa'amakim*, pp. 20–21: "One has to see things from a Biblical perspective… We must sense the greatness of the hour, in its Biblical dimension…" I shall expand on this issue below.
6. See Luz, p. 142–3.

walk contrary to me... then will I also walk contrary to you" (Leviticus 26:21–24). Nahmanides explains that God, in effect, tells us, "I will leave you in the hands of chance" (Commentary on Job 36:7). Perhaps God had decided to leave His people in the hands of chance and, as a part of a fortunate accident, I was saved. If such is the case, then my salvation was a result of God acting in a contrary manner with His people, and not because He saw fit to single me out among millions!

If I positively knew that the Holy One, blessed be He, chose me, that God had singled me out for some special purpose, then such knowledge would, indeed, place a great burden upon me. I doubt that I would have been able to live up to and achieve what was expected of me. Yet, I would gladly relinquish all the wealth and riches of the world, if it were true that God had chosen to bestow His grace upon me, as an individual among millions...

I am a simple person. Nevertheless, I sensed that I had to garner all the power within me, doubling and redoubling it, in order to recompense for those who are no longer with us. This knowledge gave me the daring and courage to accomplish things that were far beyond my normal abilities.[7]

I personally feel as though the call of the prophet Haggai – "Whoever among you remains" – is directed at me personally.[8]

---

7. "Forty Years Later," p. 86.
8. Rabbi Y. Amital, "This is the Day," p. 13. Following the Yom Kippur War, Rabbi Amital – with the sensitivity of one who had "been there" – identified a similar feeling among those who returned from the frontlines, alive and healthy, using almost identical expressions: "I am being audacious in wrapping myself in a mantle that is not my own and saying something that does not apply to myself, but rather to the psychological distress of our soldiers who have just returned from the frontlines... The question that plagues them, steals their peace and disturbs them relentlessly, to the point where

The sense of mission of someone who remains and who assumes the responsibility of replacing those who did not merit to survive, is one that accompanies many Holocaust survivors.[9] Emil Fackenheim counts this as one of the commandments that obligates Jews after Auschwitz.[10] But the essence of the mission is obscure. For Rabbi Amital, the sense of mission did not become a theology, a "Divine voice commanding." The conversion of the mission in the wake of the Holocaust into a religious imperative, a "614th commandment," the "commanding voice of Auschwitz," is central to the theological discussion of many thinkers, including Fackenheim, Irving (Yitzhak) Greenberg and others.[11]

> For [Fackenheim and Greenberg], [the Holocaust] represents a fateful challenge necessitating radical change in the way Jewish faith and commitment are understood. Both seek a religious justification for the centrality of the Jewish state in Jewish life and see its establishment and exercise of power as the most authentic response to the Holocaust.[12]

it becomes a great psychological distress, is: Why is it that we returned and they did not? Those cursed shells – why did they miss us and hit them?... Dear friends! The whole search for answers is in vain... (*Eight Princes*, p. 8).

9. One of the first public expressions of this feeling was by Abba Kovner in a speech before the Jewish Brigade on July 17, 1945: "Our power of persuasion lies not in our knowledge, but rather in our testimony. Fate placed us there, in a place where no one has ever stood, facing the abyss of life and the abyss of the generations. Face to face with the horror we saw the naked truth... But how are we to convey this to the hearts of a generation that did not live through all of this?" (A. Kovner, "Mission of the Last Ones," in Y. Gutman and L. Rotkirchen (eds.), *The Holocaust of European Jewry*, Jerusalem 1973, p. 483 [Hebrew]).

10. Fackenheim, *Presence*, pp. 85–6.

11. For a summary of similar positions and for further bibliography see Luz, pp. 142–161; Gorni, pp. 52–82. For literature on Greenberg's position see Luz, note 36; for Fackenheim's position, see especially Fackenheim, *Presence*, pp. 84–89, 94–5.

12. Luz, p. 160.

Rabbi Amital does not share this view. Even when he contemplates the establishment of the State against the backdrop of the Holocaust,[13] he juxtaposes them in order to highlight the greatness of the miracle embodied in the former, or to demonstrate the measure of helplessness that characterized the latter. At most, he speaks of the State of Israel as a measure of healing for the pain caused by the Holocaust.[14] He sees no causal connection, nor reaction or command, joining the Holocaust to the establishment of the State.[15] He cannot accept the view of those who maintain that the Holocaust imposes any type of command.

3. THE ANXIETY OF SURVIVAL

Another aspect of the survival of the few and the sense of mission that it entails[16] arises from Rabbi Amital's eulogy for his students who fell in the Yom Kippur War. We mourn for each individual:

> Each is a world in his own right; each is special in his own way, each is the only one of his kind in the world – there is no one else like him.[17]

13. As we shall see later on, Rabbi Amital does this frequently.
14. A healing, but not compensation. See, for example, "Confronting the Holocaust," pp. 47–48.
15. See, for example, "Confronting the Holocaust," ibid., and elsewhere. See also below, Chapter 2. Rabbi Amital likewise refuses to accept the view that the Holocaust created any type of religious imperative. *Halakhah* is binding as a religious imperative; one's internal morality may oblige one to act in certain ways, but the Holocaust cannot create a religious imperative.
16. Anxiety for the lives of the survivors is the initial expression of the sense of mission. See Luz; Schweid, *Wrestling*, pp. 190–3.
17. *Eight Princes*, p. 8. See also *HaMa'alot MiMa'amakim*, p. 29: "Perhaps it is especially important to eulogize individuals, in order to inculcate within ourselves the consciousness that this is not a matter of numbers. We are speaking not of numbers, but of worlds…"

While each individual loss in Israel's wars is terrible in its own right, it is doubly poignant that each victim is a member of a nation that had nearly been wiped out a short time before. The survival of the few also creates the need to protect fiercely every one of those survivors and their descendants:

> It is difficult for mortal lips to mention numbers. The number is great, mighty and cruel. It is cruel sevenfold when we remember that these are losses to a "nation of survivors of the sword" (Jeremiah 31:1). Each of its sons is one who "remained on his own" (Genesis 44:20). Each one inscribed for life is among those who "survives in Zion and lives on in Jerusalem" (Isaiah 4:3).[18]

The very fact of existence, and zealous protection of it, becomes a mission. The concern for the continued existence of the Jewish People appears frequently in Rabbi Amital's writings.[19] If we return to the Book of Micah, chapter 5, we encounter the mission imposed on "the small one among the thousands of Judah," a mission of communal leadership: "From you shall come forth for Me [he who is] to be ruler in Israel" (Micah 5:1). The sense of being a communal leader by virtue of being a Holocaust survivor, accompanies Rabbi Amital. He has stated this explicitly:

---

18. *Eight Princes,* p. 8.
19. For example, in a sermon dealing with Jacob and the forefathers, Rabbi Amital speaks of Jacob's sense of mission and responsibility, where he is conscious of the fact that each of his actions will influence the fate of the Jewish People in the future. In the midst of his speech, Rabbi Amital demands, "He has to survive and be saved, for he will bring to the world Issachar, Joseph, and the King Messiah!" (Rabbi Y. Amital, "The Significance of Jacob's words to Esau," *Alon Shevut Bogrim* 5, 1994, p. 22). This leads to a discussion of Jacob's sense of personal responsibility, and touches on the issue of existence itself: the obligation to be saved and to survive.

I am a Holocaust refugee, and I sensed a need to say
what I have said because I feel that I represent here a
large community that is disappearing.[20]

* * *

Survival anxiety, with its conscious source in the fear of destruction
in the Holocaust, is reflected in Rabbi Amital's ideological and political positions. The fear for existence itself that was reawakened
during the period leading up to the Six Day War is mentioned in
several of his discourses from that time:[21] "That deep fear that surrounded the entire House of Israel prior to the Six Day War, for
our very existence – a fear in which associations of Auschwitz and
Majdanek were intertwined..."[22] This fear does not subside over
time; it leads one to seek a stable existence. Even in quieter and more
peaceful times, there is a threat to one's very survival:

> That fear has not yet completely passed, even with the
> feeling of relief that accompanies our victories... It is
> simply repressed... into the innermost soul. Our gen-
> eration still lacks a sense of stability in the assurance of
> our survival. Somewhere in our hearts there still flick-
> ers the fear of a different political constellation, the fear

20. A. Bender, "We Cannot Say That our Hands Have Not Spilled This Blood,"
    Ma'ariv, November 12, 1995, special edition of *Ma'ariv Today*, p. 6.
21. See below. This sense of fear would be mentioned many years later. See for
    example: Rabbi Y. Amital, "Burst Forth and Sing Together, O Ruins of
    Jerusalem" (discourse on Jerusalem Day 1995), *Alon Shevut Bogrim* 9, 1996,
    pp. 97–101 [Hebrew]; translation archived at http://www.vbm-torah.org/
    yyerush/yerush57.htm. It is instructive to note Rabbi Amital's words at the
    end of this discourse: the great fear of a second Holocaust that prevailed on
    the eve of the Six Day War brought about a situation whereby the victory
    and salvation of that war atoned somewhat for the great *hillul ha-Shem* of
    the Holocaust.
22. *HaMa'alot MiMa'amakim*, pp. 90; these words were uttered on Hannukah
    1967–8.

of unexpected developments in the mentality of the enemy and his military preparedness... and there is a muted inner feeling that this sense of stability can be attained... only if we see ourselves as a link in that great chain of the historical Israel, whose eternity is assured under any conditions, so long as the heaven and earth exist. Only from the perspective of continuity can we attain a genuine feeling of stability...[23]

The anchoring of a sense of stability requires that we enlist all of Jewish history, connecting the frail link of our generation to the infinite chain that stretches into the past and into the future, the chain whose eternity "is assured under any conditions, so long as the heaven and earth exist" – nothing less.[24] Another way of gaining a sense of stability is identifying the State of Israel as a stage in a redemptive process. Only an irreversible process of redemption can provide the survivors with a sense of security. Such a definition harnesses the State of Israel to an assurance of existence, and may lend it a sense of permanence and security. Such a definition may heal the scar left by the fear for survival. Only the knowledge that we are on the road to redemption can bring relief to the "survivors of the sword."[25] Note that there is no theological explanation or historical understanding of the Holocaust here; there is mention only of a scar and of healing.

23. Ibid.
24. Many years later, Rabbi Amital would declare of the State of Israel that "Existence beyond fifty years is permanent existence" ("Discourse for Independence Day [1998]," *Daf Kesher* vol. 7, p. 240 [Hebrew]; archived at http://www.etzion.org.il/dk/1to899/652daf.htm). The sense of stability that arises from these words testifies to the need for it.
25. *HaMa'alot MiMa'amakim*, p. 47. Later on, in my treatment of the relationship between the Holocaust and the establishment of the State of Israel, I shall elaborate on this subject.

The sense of fear for survival, with its source in the Holocaust, also guides Rabbi Amital's political views:

A Jew who lived through the Holocaust, a Jew who has lived through five wars – the War of Independence, the Sinai Campaign, the Six Day War, the Yom Kippur War and the Lebanon War, not counting the War of Attrition – may be forgiven for fearing yet another war.[26]

It appears that the fear for national survival, grounded in the destruction of the Holocaust, determined several of Rabbi Amital's positions following the Six Day War: the identification with the promise of continuity, which facilitates a genuine feeling of stability; the need to locate our era on the time continuum of redemption, which provides the assurance that there is no turning back in the process of redemption; the need to provide continued motivation for Israel's struggle, beyond the belief that "there is no choice;" and later even the adoption of a realist political stance in order to assure survival.

The desperate search for stable and assured survival as a healing for the Holocaust pertains not only to physical survival, but also to the continuity of tradition, which creates a stable identity in the transition from the older generation to the younger one. This chain was severed, and the younger generation seeks a stable identity definition. In disputing Rabbi Zvi Yehudah Kook, when Rabbi Amital claimed that Nahmanides' statements concerning the settling of the land are mentioned nowhere in all of Rabbi Avraham Y. Kook's writings (except for one instance, in a discussion related to the Sabbatical year),[27] he explains as follows the dependence of those who follow Rabbi Zvi Yehudah on the words of Nahmanides:

26. "Cry of an Infant," p. 84.
27. "Not Everything," pp. 97–98. Elsewhere Rabbi Amital speaks of this claim as follows: "This is one of the clearest facts that proves that Rabbi Zvi Yehudah's path is different from my own. All of his teaching is built on this

In the wake of the severance in the fundamental Jewish continuity of the nation as a result of the Holocaust, the new generation lacks the rootedness that nourished their forefathers. For them, everything now has to be re-examined with a wretched sense of insecurity. Anything that is not discussed explicitly in the *Shulhan Arukh* is difficult to integrate properly into one's inner world, and especially one's Torah world. Concerning the issue of *Eretz Yisrael*, in contrast, there is a famous comment by Nahmanides emphasizing that the *mitzvah* of settling the land applies at all times.[28]

This is Rabbi Amital's explanation for the dependence on and careful adherence to the formal written *Halakhah*: the younger generation's need for a stable identity, in a world in which the continuity of generations has been ripped apart.

The connection between Rabbi Amital's personal biography and his positions is overt, conscious and stated explicitly in a variety of contexts. For instance, in speaking of *hesder* yeshivahs, which alternate Torah study with military service, as a first-choice option for religious youth, he states:

...It as a shame and disgrace when people say that because of fifteen months of involvement in the *mitzvah* of military service one cannot become a great Torah scholar. I once had friends who gave much more than fifteen months to the Nazis, and still became Torah

Nahmanides... The Rabbi [Rabbi Avraham Yitzhak ha-Kohen Kook] was aware of this [comment of] Nahmanides, as we see from his discussions with the Ridbaz concerning *Shemittah* – but he was silent" (transcript of discourse for Hannukah 1996, p. 3). This excerpt is taken from a transcript of the discourse, but was omitted from the printed version ("Religious Significance"). A similar statement appears in *Alon Shevut Bogrim* 8, 1996, p. 137. See also *Alon Shevut Bogrim* 9, 1996, p. 178.

28. "Guardian of Israel," p. 50 (discourse for Independence Day 1993).

giants. What happened to them in Europe? And suddenly now if one gives twenty months to the army it is
impossible to become a Torah scholar?[29]

29. "Understand the Years," p. 137. There are many other examples, e.g., his
discourse for Jerusalem Day 1973 (*HaMa'alot MiMa'amakim,* p. 79). Rabbi
Amital compares the sense of danger at that time to the sense of danger preceding the Six Day War, a comparison that is found in many of the descriptions of that time: "That sense of 'You have kept me alive from descend-
ing into the abyss' (Psalms 30:4) must be seen against the backdrop of the
Holocaust. For the first time since the Second World War, there was a feeling
in Israel of confrontation with the Holocaust. In the Eichmann trial, they
reminded us of the Holocaust. But the real confrontation with the Holocaust,
one that brought it into Israeli consciousness, came in the days that preceded
the Six Day War. Those were days of telegrams and telephone calls from all
over the world with proposals to transfer the children to safe places overseas"
(ibid., pp. 80–81). Elsewhere, he says: "Two pictures arise before my eyes: on
the one hand, a vision of tens of thousands of Jews – young, old, women,
children – crammed into cattle cars, being led to the valley of death; on the
other hand – an IDF parade at the foot of the wall in the reunited Jerusalem
on Independence Day 1968" (ibid., p. 85). At times it is difficult to ignore
the autobiographical background to Rabbi Amital's outlook in general. See,
for example: ibid., p. 74.

Chapter two

The God Who is Revealed Through Historical Events

I. POSITIONS WITHIN RELIGIOUS ZIONISM

REMEMBRANCE of the past and recognition of God's activity in history are an integral part of Jewish experience and Jewish tradition.[1] At the same time, the degree to which we are able to decode the religious significance of historical events is a question to which varying responses have been offered.[2]

The assumption that one may detect traces of Divine activity in history, and that the religious significance of historical events may be decoded and interpreted, is one of the outstanding characteristics of the Religious Zionist cultural climate in Israel. In this regard, Rabbi Amital has been one of the leading spokesmen of Religious Zionism, expressing "a great faith... in the continuous Divine intervention in the paths of world history, in the hand of God that guides the spiritual movements of the Israelite nation..."[3]

1. I shall discuss this at greater length below.
2. A diachronic cross-section of the attitude of Jews towards history and remembrance from several perspectives has been drawn up by Y.H. Yerushalmi, *Zakhor*.
3. *HaMaʼalot MiMaʼamakim*, p. 115.

After World War 1, Rabbi Kook wrote the following lines in a letter that has been quoted frequently by his followers:[4]

> We are a nation that knows the letters in the Book of God... like the book of Creation and the history of the world and of mankind; we also know how to read – through select individuals and their light that lives among us – that blurred script of the causes of these events, which all the magicians and conjurers, wise men and professors could not... In our heart of hearts there is not the slightest doubt concerning the wondrous precision of the Supreme Wisdom in the processes of the evolution of history.[5]

Historical events are an open book; the writing is admittedly blurred, but there are those who are able to read it: "select individuals and their light that lives among us." This way of thinking characterizes many of Rabbi Kook's disciples, and their students in turn. They, as well as other Religious Zionist leaders, contemplated the historical reality, read the script, whether clear or "that blurred script of the causes of these events," and understood its meaning; they looked at their historical situation and saw within in "the imprints of the revealed End"[6] and the signs of "the beginning of the Redemption."[7]

This idea is applied by Rabbi Zvi Yehudah ha-Kohen Kook in relation to the Holocaust as well. Here, too, in his opinion, it is possible to "encounter... the Master of the Universe:"

---

4. For example: Aviner, "Holocaust;" Aviner, *Waves*, p. 222; Tau, pp. 12–13.
5. RAYH Kook, *Letters*, II, #737, p. 334 [Hebrew].
6. RAYH Kook, *Letters*, II, #308, p. 344 [Hebrew].
7. A list of sources in which rabbis and other thinkers have pointed to various signs as showing that we are now in a "time of [Divine] visitation" has been drawn up by Rabbi S. Aviner, "Clarifications Regarding [the Oath] 'Not to Ascend the Wall,'" *Noam* 20, Jerusalem 1980, p. 8 [Hebrew]. See also the references to Rabbi Kook's *Letters* in note 94 there.

… All of our efforts, all of our desire, are towards an encounter to some degree with the Master of the Universe… We must see what God's actions are in the progression of the generations, in the progression of the times, in the progression of the consolations, with a wholeness of thought and a wholeness of faith. "Understand the years of each generation" (Deut. 32:7) … [this means] becoming accustomed to God's mind, becoming accustomed to perceiving revelations of Divinity with consciousness and understanding.[8]

A genuine world-view and genuine faith include also an understanding of history: "Remember the days of the world; understand the years of each generation" (Deut. 32:7). [This involves] an understanding of God's revelation in the world in all spheres: the revelation of God in nature and – no less importantly – the revelation of God in history, in "the years of each generation."[9]

It appears that there are no disciples of Rabbi A.Y. Kook and of Rabbi Zvi Yehudah Kook who do not adhere to this philosophy.[10] It involves not only the commandment and the ability to examine past events after the fact and to perceive through them what was being done behind the scenes, but also the ability to know God's direction in the present and the future with some degree of certainty.[11] This trend is described as follows by Aviezer Ravitzky: "The Jew need only study well the dramatic events transpiring, on the one hand,

---

8. RZYH Kook, "Holocaust Remembrance Day" (1973), in *Discourses – Tazria Metzora, Yom HaShoah*, p. 7.
9. RZYH Kook, "The Holocaust" (1967), in *Discourses – Aharei Mot, Counting of the Omer, The Holocaust, Kedoshim, Emor*, p. 11.
10. For sources other than those already mentioned, see Ravitzky, *Messianism*, p. 128–9 and especially note 205.
11. See Aviner, *Lavi*, p. 148: "Prof. [Yeshayahu] Leibowitz often asks: 'Do we have communication from behind the [heavenly] curtain, so as to assert that now is the "beginning of the sprouting of our redemption?"' The answer is: Yes.

and the promises of the prophets, on the other to grasp the whole."[12] Among the various spokesmen of this circle, a discussion of God's direction based on an analysis of historic events is regarded as quite natural and in no need of justification.[13]

What was the source of this attention and sensitivity to his-

We do have such communication. The prophets of Israel have communication, even concerning that which is destined to be in the future, and they passed down to us the 'secret' of this communication."

It is out of such certainty that the deterministic approach, described by Ravitzky, "Fate," may develop. Such an approach assumes, first and foremost, an explanation for historical events. Anyone who believes that the statement that "the dawn has broken" is a tangible historical fact can, with the addition of certain other theological assumptions, be "certain that this beginning will grow higher and more elevated" (Filber, p. 176).

12. Ravitzky, *Messianism*, p. 128.
13. A typical example of this perception may be found in an article published by Rabbi Yoel bin-Nun more than a decade ago ("The Time for Summary and Accounting Is Here," *Nekudah* 123, 1989 [Hebrew]), which presents a broad historical perspective on the events of the twentieth century, including the history of the Zionist Movement and the State of Israel, in order to analyze the miracles that have been performed for the nation of Israel "within the intricacies of world politics," and an accounting of the moments of success and failure of the State of Israel and the Zionist Movement. Rabbi Yoel bin-Nun notes the "guile of history" or the "hand of Providence," and even attempts to answer the question, "What is the word of God that is heard from among all of these monumental changes?" He rebuffs alternative answers to this question from within Religious Zionism: the answers of Rabbi Moshe Levinger, Yehudah Etzion and Rabbi Aviner (ibid. p. 29). Another example, no less fascinating, is a booklet published by "Ma'aleh" – the Center for Religious Zionism, containing a collection of responses to the First Gulf War (Y.S. Recanati (ed.), *And You Shall Stand By Silently: An Initial Look at the Significance of the Gulf War,* Jerusalem 1991 [Hebrew]). The short time between January and March 1991, devoid of any historical perspective, was sufficient for fifteen scholars (in the spheres of Bible, literature, Rabbinic literature, and philosophy), publicists, politicians and rabbis – all from within Religious Zionism – to imbue what was going on around them with ideological and religious significance. Not all responded to the same degree and with the same enthusiasm to the ideological and theological challenge. But even the few who did not draw extensive religious and ideological understanding from the events that were still taking place around them, with facts far from attaining any status of certainty – even they saw the need to address them. It

tory among Religious Zionist thinkers? Modern historiography has undergone a process of secularization, subjecting itself to the rules of nature and the system of human causality.[14] Religious Zionist thinkers were open to the prevailing general culture and its philosophy,[15] internalized the trends of modern historiography, and adopted its output. They went a step further: following a Hegelian mode of thought,[16] they endowed history with religious significance, thereby bringing it back to theology. The products of historical research and study, accepted by Religious Zionist thinkers as part of the modern scientific reality, now became materials in the service of theology. Modern history became a new tool by means of which these thinkers could decode God's intentions.[17]

One cannot ignore a possible connection between this general trend and a world-view that assumes Divine immanence – a

is interesting to note Dr. Yosef Burg's quotation of H. Graetz: "Anyone who writes Jewish history has to believe in the 'hand of God', but to describe – he is entitled to describe only 'the finger of God'" (ibid., p. 18). I believe that this booklet testifies to the extent of the complete internalization of this approach within Religious Zionism, as its name proves.

14. See, for example, a comment by Fackenheim: "God, it seems, must be expelled from history by the modern historian, just as He is expelled from nature by the modern scientist" (Fackenheim, *Presence*, p. 5). Later on, Fackenheim addresses the question of God's presence in history in the context of the Holocaust.

15. "There is almost no Religious Zionist thinker of stature who has not studied the secular cultural and philosophical works in the original and in translation and been influenced by them" (Schwartz, *Faith*, p. 179). See also Ish-Shalom. It seems that the degree of internalization of modernity requires additional study. See Harold Fisch, *The Zionist Revolution: A New Perspective*, London 1978, p. 64 ff. See also Brown.

16. See, for example, Ravitzky, *Messianism*, p. 111–2; Shlomo Avineri, *The Making of Modern Zionism: The Intellectual Origins of the Jewish State*, New York 1981, pp. 192–195. Hegelian thought (whether first-, second- or third-hand) left its mark on the historical perception of Rabbi Kook, who was conscious of secular culture. See Ish-Shalom, p. 262 note 139, pp. 293–4 note 52.

17. A reason for the sensitivity to history displayed by Religious Zionist thinkers is provided by Ravitzky, *Freedom*, p. 109. The process is a complex one, and I hope to address it elsewhere.

philosophy that is common to several guiding lights of Religious Zionism.[18] Such a connection may provide an internal, religious motive for delving into history. The profane world with its nature and history are sanctified and elevated, thereby becoming a worthy subject for theological study. It follows from the idea that God is tangibly present in all of reality that a penetrating examination of the process of current history – or of nature – will reveal its hidden Godliness.[19]

Dov Schwartz maintains that even the few Religious Zionist philosophers who have rejected the idea of immanence operated "within the cultural-ideological climate of the immanent approach to the Divine, and its conceptual system."[20] This paves the way for them to see Divine guidance expressed in the events of history. Y. Aviad (Wolfsberg) formulates this as follows: "History… is perceived

---

18. Dov Schwartz recently claimed that Religious Zionist thought developed a theology at the center of which stands the perception of Divine immanence. In the context of our discussion, "immanence" refers to Divine presence and involvement in Creation as a whole as well as in each of its components. This is not just a one-time presence (such as the act of *creatio ex nihilo*, or the presence that is to be found in relationships of cause and effect), but rather a permanent, internal presence and continuous involvement. This definition is proposed by Schwartz, *Faith*, p. 64. See also Schwartz's works, *Land*; *Religious Zionism*. In his view, the practical ideology of Religious Zionism is consolidated and molded in the wake of defined theological assumptions. Even without analyzing Schwartz's basic assumption, his indication of the connection between Religious Zionism and the assumption of Divine immanence remains relevant to our discussion.

19. Whether by this we mean an involvement that "expands God's presence to the point of internal propulsion of the process," a perception that Schwartz views as being common to Rabbis Reines, Amiel, Uziel and Soloveitchik (Schwartz, *Faith*, p. 113), or whether we mean a perception that stretches "Divine involvement to the end, making the whole world exist within the Divine"(ibid., an approach which, to Schwartz's view, is supported by the schools of Rabbi A.Y. Kook and his disciples, Rabbi David Ha-Kohen (the "Nazir"), Rabbi Y.M. Harlap, and also to some extent Rabbi Zvi Yehudah Kook, and one that has influenced various thinkers amongst the leadership of *Ha-Po'el Ha-Mizrahi*, such as Bernstein, Aminoah and Shragai).

20. Ibid., p. 112.

by our nation as full of Divine hints, as the place of the revelation of Divine Providence."[21] It goes without saying that those views that assume a "strong" Divine immanence, such the followers of Rabbi Kook, discover therein a sensitivity to events and their interpretation. The same conclusion is deduced, in a different context, by Ravitzky, with regard to both the "Rabbi Kook school"[22] and Habad:

> Let us assume that for whatever reasons a new sensitivity to history has awakened in the heart of the faithful believer; he is newly attentive to current events. Shall he not now extend the stage of religious drama to these [spheres] as well? Shall he not now expect to discover immanence and sanctity and [Divine] realization in history too?[23]

However, this connection does not necessarily follow, and it is possible to adapt historical matter for theological use even without the assumption of Divine immanence. In this regard, Rabbi Amital seems to stand apart from most of the great Religious Zionist teachers. Rabbi Amital has never had any need for immanent philosophies,[24] but at the same time he has been among the most important Religious Zionist teachers who have adapted historical matter for theological use.

It should be noted that one of the ideological mainstays of Religious Zionist circles rests on the interpretation of a current event:

21. Rabbi Y. Aviad (Wolfsberg), *Thoughts on the Philosophy of History*, Jerusalem 1958, p. 230 [Hebrew]. Quoted by Schwartz, ibid., p. 74.
22. Which maintains "a monotheistic philosophy that tends towards a pantheistic interpretation" (Rabbi A.Y. Kook, *Lights of Holiness*, II, Jerusalem 1988, p. 399 [Hebrew]), according to which the world has no independent reality of its own, separate from the Divine.
23. Ravitzky, *Freedom*, p. 109. The article was first published in 1997, entitled "Messianic Myth and Historical Drama," in D. Ohana and R. Westreich (eds.), *Myth and Remembrance*, Jerusalem-Tel Aviv 1997, p. 88 ff [Hebrew].
24. See below, note 89.

the success of the agricultural settlement of the land is testimony
to the "revealed end."[25]

2. RABBI AMITAL'S POSITION: THE
SEARCH AND THE WITHDRAWAL

a. The Search

Rabbi Amital has been one of the most outstanding representatives
of the outlook described above. For years, he portrayed God as operating through historical events and being revealed through them.
In this view, God's direct activities in history leave signs that may
be identified and revealed. It is possible to interpret and understand
the events that take place here in our world, and to learn from them
about the direction in which the God of history is operating:

> The Torah and the prophets command us incessantly
> to investigate [the meaning of events]. This is also a
> natural intellectual requirement for a person of faith.
> Our Sages define a person who makes no attempt to
> penetrate the true meaning of events that happen to
> him as one who is dead: "A wicked person during his
> lifetime is considered as one who is dead, for he sees the
> sun rise but does not recite the blessing, '…Who creates
> light;' he sees the sun set but does not recite the blessing,
> '…Who brings the evening'"(*Midrash Tanhuma, Ve-Zot
> ha-Berakhah* 7)…[26]
> We have a special obligation to see things in a

25. In accordance with the words of Rabbi Abba (*Sanhedrin* 98a): "There is no
more obvious sign of redemption than this, as it is written, 'As for you, O
mountains of Israel – you shall give forth your branches and bear your fruit
for My nation Israel' (Ezekiel 36:8)."
26. *HaMa'alot MiMa'amakim*, p. 11 (discourse on November 20, 1973). This idea
had been formulated already in 1960; see ibid. p. 110.

dual light… to see in the simple sense, and to see in the sense of understanding, of perceiving the hidden facet, the potential lying within that which is revealed in actuality.[27]

The above midrash, which talks about Divine revelation within the sphere of nature, is broadened to encompass Divine revelation within the sphere of history. Such revelation is to be found in the mysteries of history; it is hidden behind the revealed aspects of events. A dual examination allows us to access the theological significance of things that happen, and to identify the intentions of the Creator Who watches over the entire world. History is a Divine utterance that requires decoding and may be decoded. It is the locus of the decisive encounter between God and man. This encounter is man's challenge. The demand that one ponder Creation is extended further, to a demand that one ponder life's events:

> One's psychological attitude towards life's events – from the point of view of their Divine significance, as revelations of Providence – is the true test of the depth of a Jew's religiosity.[28]

We are able and obligated to investigate the layer of meaning that is covered up and concealed behind the revealed reality. This path is laid down already in the Bible:[29]

---

27. *HaMa'alot MiMa'amakim*, p. 54. Rabbi Amital comments further: "Sometimes people discover God at a time of action or activity, sometimes God is revealed to them through salvation, and sometimes people come to a recognition of their Creator through great events of faith" ("A Lecture on the *Ner Mitzvah* of the Maharal," *Alon Shevut* 5:12, 1974, p. 44.)
28. *HaMa'alot MiMa'amakim*, p. 110.
29. As already noted by Yerushalmi, pp. 8–9, 96–97 and elsewhere. See also *Kuzari* 1:25.

Things must be seen in a Biblical perspective... We must see the greatness of the hour, in its Biblical dimension...[30]

In the world of the Bible, human eyes may perceive the Divine meaning of events. Seeing things in a "Biblical perspective" means viewing the world through prophetic eyes. The prophets interpreted the history of their time, understanding its significance and the Divine intention that it embodied. The expression "seeing things in a Biblical perspective"[31] is clarified when we regard it against the backdrop of the return to the physical land of the Bible[32] and the

30. *HaMa'alot MiMa'amakim*, pp. 20–21. See also further quotes below, and those adjacent to note 51 below.

31. Ibid., as well as in other excerpts, some of which are mentioned below, and others adjacent to note 51 below.

32. The sense of "returning to the Bible" also has ramifications concerning the status of Bible study and the way in which it is taught in yeshivahs and the Religious Zionist educational institutions. Yeshivat Har Etzion has made a great contribution in this regard. The yeshivah has developed ground-breaking methods of studying and teaching Bible, with the approval of the Roshei Yeshivah and with their stamp of legitimacy. The institutional expression of this change is to be found in the journal *Megadim*, published by the Yaacov Herzog Teachers' College affiliated with Yeshivat Har Etzion. Rabbi Amital describes the innovation in Bible study as "an integral part of Torah study which has brought about a revolution in our yeshivah world," with full knowledge that this innovation originated in the yeshivah that he himself founded and led ("Understand the Years," p. 138). See also U. Simon, "The Status of the Bible in Israeli Society: From National Legend to Existential Reality" [Hebrew], *Yeri'ot* 1, Jerusalem 1999, adjacent to note 25. What appears to Simon as a cautious and hesitant change, is a great change for a yeshivah that regards itself – explicitly and implicitly – as part of the "yeshivah world," a change requiring rabbinic legitimization. Decades after the beginning of this change, the question of Bible study in yeshivahs is still controversial. See recently Rabbi A. Bazak, "The Ways of God Are Straight – and the Righteous Shall Walk in Them" [Hebrew], *Daf Kesher* #845 (2002), archived at http://www.etzion.org.il/dk/1to899/845daf.htm. For criticism from a different perspective concerning the ramifications of returning to the literal meaning of the biblical text, see M. Meir, "Talmud Out – Bible In," *Meimad* 4, 1995 [Hebrew]. See also Luz, p. 370 in original Hebrew text.

mindset of active state-building. The Zionist movement changed the Jewish attitude towards national-political activity – including war. Previously, war occupied a peripheral place in Jewish consciousness, in the memory of the distant past or in prophetic visions of the future. It had no relevance for the Jewish present;[33] it was perceived as "the art of Esau."[34] The wars of our generation have brought us back to our "history." Not only are they grounded in the vision of redemption; they also relive our biblical past. A nation living in its land and fighting for it represents a biblical reality.

In a discourse delivered to the yeshivah on November 20, 1973, about three weeks after the end of the Yom Kippur War, Rabbi Amital stated:

> War is a biblical phenomenon... In war, one has to perceive the biblical dimension... Chapters of Psalms take on a meaning that is not new to them; they once again assume their original significance. After all, King David waged war... After two thousand years of exile, they once again breathe the air of the Bible.[35]

In the same discourse, Rabbi Amital attempts to answer the question of the meaning, theological purpose and the place of war in the course of Jewish and human history:

> What is the significance of this war?... Everything that has happened to us up until this era confirms and strengthens the inner certainty that we indeed find

33. Rabbi Amital states this as fact: "The Bible is full of wars, but since [while we were in exile] we did not engage in war, we did not relate to them" (*HaMaʾalot MiMaʾamakim*, p. 21). What Rabbi Amital treated in November 1973 as fact had been regarded by Rabbi A.Y. Kook as the moral choice of the Jewish nation (RAYH Kook, *Orot*, p. 96). See also Luz, pp. 21–24.

34. Luz, p. 24, note 27. In addition, see Rashi, Genesis 49:5; *Midrash Tanhuma, Vayehi* 9.

35. *HaMaʾalot MiMaʾamakim*, pp. 20–21.

ourselves in the period of the beginning of the redemption… The question is asked, … What is the purpose
of war? … A question may be asked where it is possible
to give an answer.[36]

Rabbi Amital believed that it was possible to answer the question,[37] and he did so. It seemed possible to him to find the place of
current events on the continuum of the Divine process stretching
from the past into the future, from exile to redemption. He felt it
possible to find a sufficiently broad perspective to facilitate some
kind of meaningful explanation. The interpretation of events was
undertaken out of conviction and internal certainty. The daring, the
possibility and ability to provide such an immediate reaction, arose
from the fact that the answers were hewn from modes of meaning
that already existed in Religious Zionist thought. Religious Zionist
thought was formulated and adapted to the political reality as events

36. Ibid., p. 11–12. The discourse was first published in *Alon Shevut* 5:9, 1974,
p. 2 ff. Thereafter it was published again in the *HaMa'alot MiMa'amakim*
collection. The discourse was also published the same year in the journal
Morashah, vol. 7. The fact that the discourse was published over and over
seems to testify to its importance and the need for it at that time. The entire
discourse must also be understood against the backdrop of the educational
need to explain the events of the time and to give them meaning. The discourse, which was delivered at the yeshivah, was also addressed to the majority of its students who were still in uniform. The impressions of the scenes of
the war and its price were still a searing fire, and its conclusion was not yet
certain. Some of the students of the yeshivah were facing the Third Army
on both sides of the Suez Canal, while others were engaged in a war of attrition in the "Quneitra enclave." The atmosphere was one of fateful days
whose greatness and significance could not be denied. This was the atmosphere that had prevailed amongst the Israeli public in general and in the
Religious Zionist camp in particular since the Six-Day War, and which grew
stronger and matured into action in the form of the settlement of Sebastia
in the summer of that year.

37. By contrast, in response to the question of what the future holds, Rabbi
Amital commented: "That is a question that only those endowed with
prophecy can answer; we can speak only of a general process" (*HaMa'alot
MiMa'amakim*, p. 12).

unfolded, as part of the Religious Zionist world-view that treated current and historical events as an open book.

One who believed, upon examining the events of the time, that he could discern the messianic era approaching, also believed that he held the keys to understanding the historical events. Here we find expression of the confidence in the ability to interpret history and to perceive current events as "a single process, leading towards the arrival of the Just Redeemer."[38]

In his collection of discourses *HaMa'alot MiMa'amakim*, Rabbi Amital raises a word of caution and hesitation: "We lack the tools to know the Divine mysteries and to decide what the considerations, motivations and intentions of Divine Providence were."[39] But immediately he goes on to reject this reservation, and claims that "spectacles of faith" allow for a sense of inner certainty:

> Sometimes a person merits that when he observes events through spectacles of faith, the fog clears and things become focused, and he achieves a sense of inner certainty – a certainty that can not always be proven scientifically, but whose validity is not thereby diminished.[40]

Based on this view, Rabbi Amital rejects the "perception of reality as it is:"

> There are those who call for realism, to see reality as it is, claiming objectivity. They are seriously mistaken, for if one does not see what is hidden in the present concerning the future, then it is impossible to understand even that which is itself revealed. That which exists "in potential" is the realm not of prophets and visionaries,

38. Ibid., p. 9.
39. Ibid., p. 11.
40. Ibid.

but rather of those who understand the present, for the "potential" is what causes that which exists in "reality" and influences it… One has to see beyond the "reality," that which is revealed externally, to that which exists "in potential" – that which is hidden and destined to be revealed to us for the good.[41]

Past and future touch each other. The capacity for inner understanding of the present facilitates knowledge of the future. The ability to see that which exists "in potential" is a quasi-prophetic ability. The statement by the Sages that "a wise man is preferable to a prophet"[42] echoes in the words, "That which exists 'in potential' is the realm not of prophets and visionaries, but rather of those who understand the present," but here "those who understand the present" – by virtue of their understanding the present – become prophets of the future. The ability also comes from the power of faith: "Sometimes a person merits that when he observes events through spectacles of faith, the fog clears and things become focused."[43] This ability is one that is inherited:

> …This special gift, the capacity for dual vision, was handed down [by Abraham] to his children after him.[44]

Sensitivity to historical events and the desire to explain them can take the form of anxious attempts to analyze events in detail, on the assumption that an understanding of the exact details of the event facilitates an accurate revelation of God's intentions.[45]

41. Ibid., p. 54
42. *Bava Batra* 12a.
43. *HaMa'alot MiMa'amakim*, p. 11.
44. Ibid., p. 54
45. In the discourse on Independence Day following the Yom Kippur War, Rabbi Amital told his students: "In my visits to you on the various fronts, and in my meetings with senior commanders, I was bothered by a simple historical

Rabbi Amital pursued this path for many years.[46] Until the 1980's, he was one of the leading proponents of this philosophy. He propagated – both among his students and amongst the Religious Zionist public at large – the attitude that we are able to see and interpret God's direct involvement in history. With hindsight, he says of himself:

> In the past, students at the yeshivah would ask me to try and place things in the perspective of faith – how things should be perceived; how to look at victories and how, God forbid, to look at defeats.[47]

The word "meaning" is a thread that runs through Rabbi Amital's discourses when he addresses current events. The results of his efforts to explain reality and to give it meaning are scattered throughout his discourses as printed in various forums. Some were collected in his book *HaMa'alot MiMa'amakim,* which was published after the Yom Kippur War. This collection, containing articles that were written or discourses delivered in this spirit ("written words, dealing with the meaning of events and the processes of redemption"[48]), had a great impact in the years following that war. The War of Independence, the establishment of the State, the Six-Day War, the immigration of Russian Jews in the 1970s and the Yom Kippur War were all illuminated in a new light.

question, which I asked over and over…" ("A New Song," *Alon Shevut* 5:24, 1974, p. 13 [Hebrew]). I shall not enter here into a discussion of the historical details that Rabbi Amital sought to understand, nor of the theological conclusions that may be drawn from them, according to his words there.

46. The earliest writings on the subject that I was able to obtain are from the year 1960. There Rabbi Amital examines "the events of the time" from the point of view of those who believe in "constant Divine involvement in the ways of world history" (*HaMa'alot MiMa'amakim,* p. 115).

47. "Cry of an Infant," p. 85. Further on Rabbi Amital notes that today people are not satisfied with theoretical religious guidance, but rather demand of Rabbis practical instructions.

48. *HaMa'alot MiMa'amakim,* p. 9.

b. The Withdrawal

In a discourse delivered in the first weeks of the Lebanon War, Rabbi Amital stated:

> There are times when it is difficult to see the hand of God in the events surrounding us, in the stories that fill the media, and there are times when God's hand is seen clearly in events, and one need not rely on verses and *midrashim*.[49]

One can open a newspaper, listen to the news, and see the hand of God. Despite his hesitations, reservations and awareness of the limitations of his perspective ("We are too close to the events; we lack the proper perspective to judge them"), Rabbi Amital comes back to the obligation to observe the hand of God in history:

> We are obligated to see God's hand guiding the heart of kings, ministers and generals in their plans for war, just as we must see God's hand on the battlefield. We must see God's hand in the various political situations of the countries around us and of the superpowers, which have eased the war for us considerably.[50]

As far as I am able to establish, this was Rabbi Amital's last explicit utterance of this sort, concerning our ability to understand the Divine intention in history. In recent years, he has become increasingly reserved in his interpretation of historical events.

It seems that, after a prolonged gestation, the Holocaust shattered his interpretation of history. For many years, Rabbi Amital – like many other Religious Zionist leaders – believed that one could examine history from the beginning of the "return to Zion" until

---

49. "Darkness," p. 5. One cannot ignore the educational need that provided the background for this discourse.
50. Ibid., p. 6

our time, and confidently see therein the signs of the End of Days. When this certainty was stricken, his faith in the ability to read the times was undermined.

Here, examination of God's works in history reaches the boundary of human ability. The Holocaust is not an event requiring simply that we interpret its "text." That text cannot be interpreted. The awesome horror does not allow us to perceive therein the "hand of God in history" in the same way that we may observe it in any other event. The questions may be formulated in many different ways: Is faith in the God of history – the God Who is revealed in the unfolding of events – possible after the Holocaust? Did all of this come about by the hand of God? Is the very mention of such a possibility not a terrible desecration of God's Name? Perhaps there is some other gateway to understanding the Holocaust, or at least to trying to address it?

First of all, it should be noted that even during those years when Rabbi Amital maintained that God's intention and direction could be discerned in current events, he stopped short of applying this philosophy to the period of the Holocaust. It would seem that the obligation to examine history includes the Holocaust: this, too, was a historical event, worthy of study in order that we may understand its meaning. And, as in other historical events, God is the address. Even if we cannot understand its full significance, it would seem nevertheless that we are not exempt from searching, examining and addressing the phenomenon:

We have to look at [the Holocaust] in a Jewish light, in a biblical light: "If you are obedient and you listen – you will eat of the good of the land; if you refuse and you rebel – you will be devoured by the sword" (Isaiah 1:19–20)… There can be no doubt that God did what He did with deliberate calculation.[51]

The Holocaust would appear to be a phenomenon that we are obligated to examine and whose meaning we must decode. The mode of thinking according to which historical events reveal God's

---

51. "A World Built," p. 27.

intentions should seemingly apply here, too. Anyone who claims to hear a Divine statement through history must grapple with the meaning of this "text," too, and to reveal its secret:

> I know that the Holocaust addresses not only this gen-
> eration but also the generations to come, but I would
> like to see a Jewish reaction in this generation too…
> We grew up during that period, and we believe – and
> this idea is spoken about at length in Hassidut – that
> every generation, every person, has a special task. My
> test of faith is different than Maimonides' test of faith.
> The grappling and the searching – that is my problem,
> although I know that I am not capable of reaching a fi-
> nal conclusion, but I search incessantly: What did God
> want of us? Where have I failed? What can I do?
>
> The searching allows me to live with this prob-
> lem. If I do not search, if I do not grapple – this event
> will be forgotten. This event cannot remain forever
> only as something experiential. It must occupy all the
> intellectual powers… This grappling is part of me, and
> it must be the initial reaction that comes after the
> Holocaust.[52]

The sense of obligation, and perhaps also the internal yearn-
ing of "Show me Your ways" (Exodus 33:13), bring Rabbi Amital to
examine the Holocaust and to try to understand its meaning, specifically because of the magnitude of the event and its uniqueness.
He gives heartfelt expression to the desperate search for meaning:
"If only we would be able to understand the thinking of our Father
in Heaven after forty years. If only we would grasp something."[53]
Together with the quest for meaning, there is also a consciousness

52. Ibid., p. 27–28.
53. "Forty Years Later," p. 85

that there will be no answer.[54] This does not mean acceptance of the situation, but rather a living with a "nightmare."[55]

For many years, Rabbi Amital espoused two contradictory positions: first, faith in the ability and the need to interpret history and to know its meaning in order to understand God's ways, and second, the knowledge that this approach is impossible when it comes to the Holocaust – accompanied by the understanding that one cannot adopt a philosophy of history that explains every event except the Holocaust. Any attempt at an explanation of the events of our generation that does not address the Holocaust, destroys the entire explanation:

> These sorts of claims inspire a gut reaction, a natural aversion that causes me to worry less about them then about the historical and religious view that ignores the Shoah, disregards and omits it absolutely from our collective memory – which is infinitely more dangerous.[56]

Rabbi Amital is aware of the reactions of fleeing and ignoring that arise from the human inability to deal with the Holocaust: "We lack the tools to deal with the Holocaust, and therefore we ignore it."[57] It is thus, for example, that he regards the Haredi ("ultra-orthodox") world-view, which ignores the Holocaust. If the leaders of the Haredi sector were to address the Holocaust, their entire ideological system would change:

> Great leaders, among them most of the great Hassidic rebbes, rejected Zionism. In the meantime a Holocaust

---

54. "A World Built," pp. 27–28.
55. Ibid., p. 27.
56. "Confronting the Holocaust," p. 48.
57. From transcript of discourse delivered on Hannukah 1996, p. 7; omitted from printed version ("Religious Significance"). See also: "Confronting the Holocaust," p. 47.

took place, in the meantime the State was established, but [to the Haredi view] it cannot be possible that the leaders were mistaken. Rabbi Dessler, of sainted memory, was asked how it was possible that the greatest leaders of Israel were mistaken and did not instruct the Jewish public to immigrate to Israel prior to the Holocaust. He answered, "From your words I see that you believe that all the great ones of Israel, all of whose deeds were for the sake of Heaven... all of them are supposed to have made a terrible mistake. God forbid that such a thing be in Israel! It is forbidden even to listen to words like these, let alone to say them."[58] [In Rabbi Dessler's view,] although reality stares us in the face, we do not have the ability to state that they were mistaken. The conclusion that arises from his approach is that we do not understand what took place, but the religious leaders were certainly not mistaken...

The correct answer, and one which Rabbi Dessler himself also knew, is that no one foresaw – nor was anyone capable of foreseeing – the Holocaust. The greatest religious leaders were not capable of foreseeing the Holocaust; they were not prophets, and we could not expect this of them. The Gemara (*Bava Kama* 52a) teaches: "When the Holy One is angry at the nation of Israel, He blinds their leader." The Holy One prevented them from seeing and preparing for what was going to happen. However, even if we say that there was a historical mistake – is their greatness thereby damaged? R. Yohanan ben Zakkai, who handed Jerusalem over to the Romans,[59] and R. Akiva, who declared Bar

58. Dessler, *Strive*, vol. I, p. 217.
59. Rabbi Amital's words here were presented in an oral discourse. The historical image that he appears to have before him is depicted in the Babylonian Talmud, *Gittin* 56b, and the words of Rabbi Yosef there concerning R.

Koziba as the Messiah and was one of his arms-bearers, as described by Maimonides – is their greatness impaired?![60]

Even the ideology that emanates from the school of Rabbi Kook goes awry in the face of the Holocaust, for Rabbi Kook did not foresee the Holocaust:

> One of the things that prevents us from understanding the teachings of Rabbi Kook is that people are afraid to state openly that there are things that Rabbi Kook did not foresee, and this in and of itself does not diminish his greatness. Rabbi Akiva, the greatest rabbi of the period of the Mishnah, believed that Bar Kokhba was the Messiah, and he was mistaken, but nevertheless he remains Rabbi Akiva. It is said that Rabbi Zvi Yehudah Kook believed that his father's essay, "*Ma'amar ha-Dor*," is a statement for all generations... He said so many wise things, so his greatness is not diminished if he also uttered one mistake...
>
> We have to know that "*Ma'amar ha-Dor*" does not speak to our generation! Rabbi Kook believed that within fifty years the Messiah would come, and anyone who reads his books cannot understand him in any other way. And behold, we have not merited his coming, and nevertheless Rabbi Kook remains the greatest Jewish thinker perhaps since the time of Maimonides. We have to remove this obstruction and know that there are things that he did not foresee, just as he did not foresee the Holocaust, for example.

Yohanan ben Zakkai: "He turns back wise men and makes their knowledge into foolishness" (Isaiah 44:25). Rabbi Amital reads the narrative through the eyes of Rabbi Yosef.

60. Transcript of a discourse delivered on Hannukah 1996, p. 2.

> Rabbi Kook was not a prophet. He tried to fore-
> see where certain [socio-historical] processes were lead-
> ing, but he was not a prophet who could see what was
> hidden in the future...
>
> We have to know that there are things that Rabbi
> Kook did not foresee, but nevertheless he remains Rabbi
> Kook.[61]

Any ideology, world-view or vision of the future that sees history as being divinely guided, yet does not take the Holocaust into
account, is guilty of ignoring the Holocaust and hiding it from view.
But, on the other hand, it is impossible to offer any explanation!
Rabbi Amital is neither able nor prepared to provide an explanation for the Holocaust, nor is he prepared to fit it into any ideology, world-view or causal chain. Therefore, during the course of the
years, he has tended increasingly towards the direction of doubt in
the very ability to explain God's ways in history.

Rabbi Amital dares to say: "I was mistaken, we were mistaken,
Rabbi Kook was mistaken, the leaders of Religious Zionism and of
the Haredi world were mistaken." The Holocaust confounded the
entire ideological system and forces us into a renewed evaluation
of our religious world-view. Just as he claimed that it is impossible
for us to base our Divine service on the principle of gratitude in a
period that witnessed the greatest destruction in the history of the
Jewish nation,[62] so he claims that it is impossible to maintain either
a Religious Zionist or Haredi ideology and ignore the Holocaust.

Rabbi Amital has retreated and withdrawn from the path he
had followed for so many years, according to which it is possible to
discern the God Who is revealed in the events of the times and to
uncover His intentions. Rabbi Amital concedes that what he sought
all these years, and that which his teachers sought, may have been

61. Rabbi Amital's words during a panel discussion: "The Significance of
    Rabbi Kook's Teachings for Our Generation," *Alon Shevut Bogrim* 8, 1996,
    pp. 136–137.
62. "Confronting the Holocaust."

a mistake; he declares, as it were, "Just as I received reward for the pursuit, so will I receive reward for withdrawing from it."[63]

Several times during recent years, Rabbi Amital has raised the possibility of being mistaken in identifying our times as "the beginning of the flowering of our redemption." Despite the fact that "the return of the nation of Israel to the land of Israel is a phenomenon that has no parallel in the world"[64] and represents "the fulfillment – even only partially – of the prophetic vision,"[65] the identification of our reality as the reality of redemption is not certain:

> Gentlemen, it may be that all those who spoke about the beginning of the flowering of our redemption were mistaken. It is possible that the students of the Vilna Gaon were mistaken, it may be that the students of the Ba'al Shem Tov were mistaken, perhaps the students of Rabbi Akiva Eiger were mistaken when they spoke about the beginning of the flowering of our redemption, as described in their books. It may be that Rabbi Kook was mistaken, it may be that Rabbi Harlap was mistaken. Rabbi Akiva, the greatest of the *Tannaim*, was also mistaken.[66]

It is no coincidence that Rabbi Amital selects Rabbi Akiva as an example of someone who was mistaken. The similarity between Rabbi Akiva's interpretation of the events of his time as having messianic significance, when he declared that Bar Kokhba had "the status of the King Messiah,"[67] and the interpretation of reality by Rabbi Amital and other Religious Zionist leaders, causes him to show a special interest in Bar Kokhba and Rabbi Akiva. But the similarity in the style of interpretation in understanding "the intricacies of

63. *Pesahim* 22b.
64. "Cry of an Infant," p. 85.
65. Ibid.
66. Ibid.
67. Jerusalem Talmud, *Ta'anit* 4:5.

Jewish history," and within it the identification of "one of the stages in the messianic process," is equally relevant:

> How, then, could Rabbi Akiva have mistaken [Bar Kokhba] for the Messiah? Bar Kokhba reinstated Jewish sovereignty about fifty years after the destruction of the Temple. Rabbi Akiva, with his profound understanding of the intricacies of Jewish history, knew that Jewish sovereignty and independence is one of the stages in the messianic process.[68]

The possible conclusion that arises from this identification is instructive: if Rabbi Akiva, the greatest of the *Tannaim*, was mistaken in his understanding "the intricacies of Jewish history," then Rabbi Kook could also be mistaken. It is at this point that Rabbi Amital stands and declares: I am not certain; it is possible that I was mistaken.

The fact that Maimonides declares that Rabbi Akiva was mistaken makes it easier for Rabbi Amital to say of great Jewish leaders that they were mistaken,[69] and to admit that what he himself taught to his students over the course of many years may also have been a mistake. If Rabbi Akiva could err – what can we say of ourselves? When a prophecy concerns the past, its interpretation is certain, for God's words are true,[70] but its realization in the future is not deterministic. Even if everything is divinely foreseen, we still have free choice. The realization of the vision of the future contained in the prophecy is dependent on human behavior:

---

68. "Sing to Him," p. 56. This discourse was delivered on Independence Day 1996.
69. It is not an easy statement to make in a world in which the opinions of leading Torah sages carry special weight, and in which even a minority opinion is considered as representing "the words of the living God." See Rabbi Amital's comments in *HaMa'alot MiMa'amakim*, p. 108 ff., and compare with his article, "Da'at Torah."
70. "A prophet does not err" ("Cry of an Infant," p. 85).

Anyone who thinks that a prophet's prophecy is independent of the spiritual conduct of the Children of
Israel does not understand what prophecy is.[71]

This is not a description of religious positions from a distance,
but rather the adoption of a religious position by someone for whom
such a position fills all of his being: as a person, as a *rosh yeshivah*
and as a participant in public leadership. Rabbi Amital is prepared
to pay a heavy price for this.[72] The certainty in explaining reality as
being guided step-by-step by God Himself was important to Rabbi
Amital, not only because it is healing for Holocaust survivors, but
also because it facilitates a sense of Divine presence. But Rabbi
Amital has reconsidered. The fundamental religious desire, "One
thing I ask … to see the goodness of God" (Psalms 27:4–13), is not
openly realized in the historical dimension.

3. BETWEEN THE EXTREMES

The range of positions adopted by believing Jews concerning God's
relationship with the world in general and the Holocaust in particular can be depicted schematically on a continuum, whose one
extreme represents the view that the Holocaust took place through
direct Divine involvement, and whose other extreme claims that the
Holocaust was a "hiding of God's face."[73]

---

71. Ibid. Rabbi Amital makes a similar statement in his article, "Facing the
    Challenge." There are Religious Zionist thinkers who believe that the process
    is deterministic and irreversible, and who maintain that the fact that we are
    now in the period of the third redemption is certain. See Ravitzky, *Messianism*,
    especially chapter 3.
72. Even a personal price, too, but that subject lies beyond the scope of this
    work.
73. For a range of additional religious views concerning the Holocaust, see for
    example Michman, "Faith," pp. 341–350; Schweid, "Orthodox;" P. Peli, "The
    Quest for a Religious Language for the Holocaust," *Topics in the Philosophy of
    the State of Israel*, Beit-El 1990, pp. 131–160 [Hebrew]; M. Werdiger; Gorni,
    chapter 2.

On one side stand those who believe that the theological-historical meaning of the Holocaust may be grasped (whether through Haredi or Religious Zionist lenses).[74] Even at the time when he claimed that one may attain an understanding of the theological meaning of historical events, Rabbi Amital rejected outright the extension of this approach to the realm of the Holocaust. He rejects the explanations of the Holocaust as part of a messianic process leading towards redemption. Even if he regards the State of Israel as a miracle and as a healing for the Holocaust, a healing for the survivors or a remedy to some degree for the great desecration of God's Name that it involved, he never accepted any causal connection whatsoever between the Holocaust and the establishment of the State.[75] Needless to say, Rabbi Amital also rejects any explanation that regards the Holocaust as a punishment for any type of sin:

> No sin, however grievous, can justify to the human
> mind the burning of tens of thousands of mothers with
> nursing infants in their arms.[76]

At the other extreme are views that have difficulty bridging the profundity of the abyss separating the evil of the Holocaust and Divine Providence. These approaches are formulated in rebellious opposition, in questioning, or in pain and sorrow.[77]

74. Concerning Haredi perspectives, see Schweid, "Orthodox," as well as his work, *From Destruction to Salvation*, Tel Aviv 1994 [Hebrew]; Piekarz; Hutner; Eliach, p. 723 ff. Concerning Religious Zionist perspectives, see below.

75. "There were those who claimed that the Holocaust was a sort of price that the Jewish People had to pay in order that the Jewish State could be established. There are those who claimed that the State of Israel is the divine compensation for the destruction of the Holocaust... These are very difficult claims, approaches that I find hard to countenance at all" ("Confronting the Holocaust," pp. 47–48).

76. "A Kaddish," p. 7. For the reader's convenience, the discourse is reprinted at the end of this volume.

77. For example: A. Donath, "A Voice From the Ashes: Wandering in Search of God," *Yalkut Moreshet* 21, 1976 [Hebrew], and the debate that took place in the wake of this article in subsequent volumes. This position can reach the

Between these two extremes, there are explanations that speak of a "hiding of God's face." While the biblical "hiding of God's face" represents a Divine response to sin (and thus, in effect, a type of "Providence"),[78] the concept has assumed a different meaning in modern Jewish thought, according to which the "hiding of God's face" is a deliberate "absence" of God and a complete transfer of responsibility to mortal hands. Responsibility for the Holocaust, in this view, rests with man. The idea of God being responsible for the Holocaust is perceived as a "desecration of God's Name." The concept of "Divine Providence," in its regular sense, cannot co-exist with the Holocaust.

Although this explanation – which "exempts" God, as it were, from responsibility – has a very strong attraction from Rabbi Amital's point of view, since it "solves" the problem of the desecration of God's Name in the Holocaust,[79] he is not tempted to adopt this approach. Nowhere does Rabbi Amital make any statement that implies in any way that God was "absent."[80] The standing in silence before the incomprehensible is filled with a sense of the Divine presence:

point of loss of faith. Rabbi Amital says of himself, "I believe in God, Whom I cannot understand" ("Confronting the Holocaust" p. 51). "Despite our lack of comprehension, despite all our questions, we nonetheless declare: *Yitgadal ve-yitkadash Shemeih rabba*, May God's great Name be elevated and sanctified" ("A Kaddish" p. 9). But he does not condemn those who lost their faith in the Holocaust (see below, chapter 3, section 4).

78. See especially E. Schweid.

79. This question has occupied Rabbi Amital extensively; I shall discuss this further.

80. Rabbi Amital does mention in one place the concept of the "hiding of God's face" in its traditional sense – and even here with reservation and hesitation: "Was I saved because God singled me out and made sure that I would not suffer the same fate as millions of others of our people? Or rather was it a mere case of chance? The verse states, 'And I will surely hide My face on that day' (Deut. 31:18). When God hides His countenance from us, it is because, as the verse tells us, 'And if you walk contrary to me... then will I also walk contrary to you (Leviticus 26:21–24). Nahmanides explains that God, in effect, tells us, 'I will leave you in the hands of chance' (Commentary on Job 36:7). Perhaps God had decided to leave His people in the hands of chance

What took place there is so unfathomable, so abnormal, incomprehensible to any logical thought, such that I could see in it only something metaphysical, some sort of "hand of God." It cannot be grasped by any logical thought. Neither logical thought nor Jewish thought… What happened there was beyond any proportion. The term "proportion" has no place here. It was so incomprehensible, so abnormal. And I saw God's hand clearly, but I did not understand what the hand meant. I was confounded and I remain confounded.[81]

I clearly experienced the hand of God during the Holocaust – only I did not understand its meaning. It was so clear – so abnormal; so unnatural; so illogical. I was not in Auschwitz, but I saw the Jews who were being taken there. I saw regiments of Germans who were not going to the Russian front, but rather guarding the trainloads of Jews that were headed to the death camps. It was against all military logic and interests. Can one possibly begin to understand such madness? I saw the hand of God in everything.[82]

The Holocaust lies outside of human comprehension. "Logical thought" and "Jewish thought" stop short, and they have no conclusion but perplexity: "I saw God's hand clearly, but I did not understand what the hand meant." On the one hand, a rejection of the explanations that speak of direct Divine involvement; on the other hand – Divine presence. The horror removes man and his logic completely from the scene, and all that remains is Divine presence.

and, as a part of a fortunate accident, I was saved. If such is the case, then my salvation was a result of God acting in a contrary manner with His people, and not because He saw fit to single me out among millions!" ("Forty Years Later," p. 88).

81. "A World Built," p. 13.
82. " Forty Years Later," p. 88

The expression, "I saw God's hand" is repeated over and over.[83] It is the same paradoxical experience that stands at the center of religiosity, "a paradox that finds perfect and repeated expression in the famous poem by Rabbi Yehudah Halevi, "God, Where shall I find You/Your place is elevated and invisible!/ And where shall I not find You/Your glory fills the world!"[84]

The opposites come together at their source, the parallel lines coalesce; but here – unlike Rabbi Yehudah Halevi's poem – both God's absence and His presence are terrifying.

This idea in Rabbi Amital's teachings finds an echo in some of Fackenheim's works,[85] but there remains a vast distance between them. Fackenheim speaks of the Holocaust as creating new religious imperatives. Rabbi Amital, in contrast, speaks of a sense of Divine presence, but does not venture a single step beyond that feeling. There is no "revelation" here accompanied by any sort of command. This point assumes even sharper focus elsewhere in Rabbi Amital's discussion of the sense of God's presence:

> I shall not go into detail, but anyone who was there saw that the events were not natural. I saw the hand of God, but not the explanation, the meaning; He spoke

83. This may be a sharper formulation of the statement of the Hassidic leader Rabbi Kalonymus Kalman Shapira, author of *The Holy Fire*, in one of his attempts to explain the reality surrounding him in the Warsaw ghetto: "It follows, then, that when we see them, God spare us, torturing and tormenting us in ways which bestow no benefit to the torturer and tormentor, just to torment us – that is an revelation of Din that is not enclothed in the natural order…" (Rabbi K.K. Shapira, *The Holy Fire*, ed. N. Polen, Northvale, NJ, 1994, p. 128).

84. Harold Fisch, *In the Secret Place on High: Paradox and Contradiction in Jewish Sources*, Ramat Gan 2001, p. 8 [Hebrew]. Fisch notes the paradox that stands at the foundation of religious expression and theological understanding.

85. See Fackenheim, "Faith;" Y. Bauer, "Points for Study," *Faith in the Holocaust*, Jerusalem 1980, p. 89 onwards [Hebrew]. The criticism leveled at Fackenheim on this issue applies to Rabbi Amital as well, for example: E. Luz p. 146–7.

to me – but I understood nothing. We saw the hand of God, we saw God's word, but what was He saying?[86]

Rabbi Amital describes a profound sense of Divine presence, with no explanation or understanding. It is a presence that shows nothing but itself. The profound experience of Divine presence that accompanies Rabbi Amital[87] does not assume Divine immanence. Perhaps this is because it is difficult to reconcile the Holocaust with a philosophy of Divine immanence. In this respect, Rabbi Amital differs from most of the Religious Zionist thinkers whose path is elucidated by Dov Schwartz.[88] In all the works published by Rabbi Amital or in his name, there is no assumption of immanence.[89]

* * *

86. "A Kaddish," p. 8.
87. In a discourse for *Selihot*, delivered on September 23, 2000, Rabbi Amital notes the sense of Divine presence that finds expression in *Selihot*: "The wholeness of a commandment is conditional upon a person feeling with all his being the presence of God… The everyday perception of Godliness in ordinary people such as ourselves is generally limited. It relates to one aspect of His Divinity – the aspect pertaining to God's relationship with us individually or collectively, aiding and supporting, healing, redeeming and uplifting or, heaven forefend, casting down, punishing, causing suffering and cutting short the lives of mortals like us" ("Discourse Preceding *Selihot*," *Daf Kesher* vol. 8, p. 415 [Hebrew]; archived at http://www.etzion.org.il/dk/1to899/777daf.htm). Further on, he discusses the feeling of God's loftiness, exaltedness, splendor, greatness and awesomeness, and the climax of the sense of His nearness expressed in the plea, "Show me Your ways"(Exodus 33:13): "We have yet to encounter a more elevated and meaningful aspect of God's Divinity. This aspect is the knowledge of God's ways concerning which Moses prayed: 'Show me Your ways'" (ibid.).
88. See notes 18–19 above, and their adjacent text. Religious Zionist philosophers and leaders operate in a climate of belief in Divine immanence. At the extreme that "stretches Divine involvement to the limit, making the entire world exist within Divinity," we find Rabbi Avraham Yitzhak ha-Kohen Kook and his disciples (Schwartz, *Faith*, p. 113). At the other extreme are views describing a "weaker" immanence, such as the type Schwartz identifies among other thinkers. The revelation of God in historical events is a reflection of the Divine essence, and one cannot take refuge in an explanation that speaks of a

Together with these and many other attempts to deal with the question of the theological meaning of the Holocaust, and the problem of theodicy in general, there is a position of "muteness" in the face of that which cannot be approached. This is formulated in an expression that represents the ultimate silence, namely, Aaron's reaction upon the death of his two sons: "*Va-yidom Aharon*" ("And Aaron was mute," Leviticus 10:3). This is not a lack of words, nor a silence following speech, but rather muteness – a verb without action, followed by stillness. It represents reconciliation with the fact that "to understand the Supreme Providence after all of this is impossible... One has no choice but to accept the incomprehensible, the unrevealed."[90] Even the prophets of Israel did not always receive answers: "I continue to exist and to live with questions for which even the prophets did not always have answers."[91] Yet there still remains the

---

"hiding of God's face," or even to find any causal mechanism that can stand between the Ultimate Cause and the events that take place in this world.

89. Rabbi Amital confirmed this when I interviewed him on September 1, 2000. On this point Rabbi Amital's position is close to that of several Haredi leaders, who maintain a religious world-view according to which "God is transcendental, and Divine Providence operates from without... the Hafetz Haim ... described God as sending prophets and kings, as exiling Israel and bestowing reward, without any hint of a Divine presence motivating all of existence with a real presence... Even Rabbi Elhanan Bunim Wasserman... describes Divine Providence as animating historical processes from without. The same applies concerning Rabbi Yoel Teitelbaum of Satmar... The same can be said of Rabbi Avraham Yishayahu Karelitz, the Hazon Ish,... and of many others" (Schwartz, ibid., pp. 181–182). Compare Brown, p. 93. Nevertheless, Rabbi Amital criticizes Haredi ideology. He expresses open surprise at Haredi views that neither experience nor express gratitude: see his, "Redemption at the Hands of Heaven," *Daf Kesher* vol. 6, pp. 514–516 (archived at http://www.etzion.org.il/dk/1to899/601daf.htm); transcript of discourse for Hannukah 1996, p. 3.

90. "Nation Before Land," p. 12. A different expression of this position is that of Job in the face of the whirlwind: "Where were you when I formed the earth? Say, if you have understanding..." (Job 38:4); "Have you pondered the expanse of the earth? Say, if you know it all" (ibid. 18).

91. "A World Built," p. 14.

longing to understand God's hand in history, as was possible concerning other events over the course of many years:

> Upon the verses, "Yet the Lord has not given you a heart to perceive, and eyes to see, and ears to hear, until this day. And I have led you forty years in the wilderness..." (Deut. 29:3–4), the Talmud comments: "From this [verse] we learn that it can take an individual forty years to know the mind of one's master" (*Avodah Zarah* 5b). The entire congregation of Israel was unable to understand the mind of its Master in heaven until forty years had passed! How much more so is it difficult to understand the mind of our Master during an era that all human logic has failed to comprehend.[92]

This, in essence, is the mood that we discussed previously:[93] the withdrawal from the attempt to understand the course of history, arising from the internalization of the limitations of knowledge, in light of the Holocaust. The limitation of knowledge that becomes apparent in the context of the Holocaust is projected onto other areas as well.

*　*　*

The quest to provide an explanation for the Holocaust is surrendered also in face of the assumption of God's morality and goodness. Without this basic assumption, there is no way of understanding the question of theodicy first posed by Abraham, and then later by Job, Jeremiah and Jews in the modern era as well.[94] This assumption

---

92. "Forty Years Later," p. 85.
93. See the end of section two of this chapter.
94. It seems that the assumption that E. Schweid attributes to modern humanism is as old as the Bible and exists among the great majority of religious thinkers of monotheistic religions. See also Statman *&* Sagi, *Religion*, p. 42. For the entire discussion see pp. 40–44.

gives rise to a position that does not attempt to cover anything up, but rather stands questioning, and finds no explanation:

> There is a different distress, namely, that of a person such as myself – to live with the Holocaust and to say, "The Rock Whose work is perfect and all His ways are righteous" (Deut. 32:4), is not simple. The problem is not one of doubts regarding faith…
>
> I grew up with Jewish thinking that says that if, in order to prolong the life of a child by a single hour, it is necessary that all of Israel desecrate the Shabbat, then we are commanded to desecrate the Shabbat for him. This is Jewish thought…
>
> I did not understand the meaning of the [Divine] hand. I was confounded and I remain confounded. As it says in Psalms (119:85), "The proud ones have dug pits for me that are not according to Your Torah." This was the opposite of Torah thought! And I have to say, and I say, (Deut. 32:4): "The Rock Whose work is perfect," and live with it. There are moments of grace where I imagine that I believe with perfect clarity, and there are moments when, as it were, I flee from Him towards Him, standing confounded, like the prophet (Habbakuk 1:13), "Your eyes are too pure to see evil and You cannot behold wickedness; why do you look at those who are treacherous and remain silent when the wicked man swallows up one who is more righteous than himself?"[95]

A religion that regards human life – even a single hour of life – as an absolute value, as a religious value, demands of God an answer to the question. The question of theodicy after the Holocaust is no different, theoretically, from the question of theodicy that

95. "A World Built," p. 14.

has existed since Abraham cried out, "Shall the judge of the whole earth not perform justice?" or any cry of protest against any kind of suffering.[96]

Our inability to decode the meaning of the Holocaust projects onto our inability to decode the meaning of any human suffering; it engenders a lack of understanding and the helplessness in the face of "regular" human suffering as well. Rabbi Amital draws a parallel between them. It is the Holocaust that taught us the turning inwards in silence in response to human suffering, and that blocked the paths of explanation for suffering in and of itself, since if one were to provide such an explanation, the Holocaust, too, would stand and await an explanation:

> We stand silent before the enormity of the Shoah, and we have no answer. "And Your faithfulness in the nights" (Psalms 92:3) – even when it is darkest, we believe that God is faithful to us. This is one of the tests with which God tries us. Despite everything, we continue to cling to God, echoing the ironic lament: "We fled from You to You." But as for a reply, there is none.
>
> Certain groups and certain rabbinical authorities presume to provide an explanation for every tragedy and disaster; they know how to answer, for example, why a certain number of children were killed in an accident. Many times, they attribute this to the sins of

96. See: "Confronting the Holocaust," pp. 46–47. These very verses are echoed by Rabbi Amital in the eulogy for his students following the Yom Kippur War: "All the searching for answers is in vain. There is no rest for the soul… This is the time to get back to basics, to a great, simple faith: 'To speak of Your mercies in the morning and Your faith in the nights' (Psalms 92:3). In the morning, we see Your word as 'true and fixed and correct and standing and straight and faithful and beloved and pleasant and lovely and good.' At night we see nothing of this. Only one thing remains: 'Your faith in the nights.' 'The Rock Whose work is perfect, for all His ways are just, a God of faith with no injustice, He is righteous and upright' (Deuteronomy 32:4)" (*Eight Princes*, p. 8).

others. Let us imagine: if we asked one of those rabbis, "You have before you two scenarios: here a million and a half children were killed, and here ten; now explain this" – what would he say? "I have an answer for the ten, but none for the 1,500,000?" Hardly. Thus, the compulsion to provide an answer for the deaths of ten children compels us to remove the Shoah, a tragedy on a scale that we cannot begin to comprehend, from our collective religious memory – for one who has not done so can never claim, for any tragedy, "I have an answer!" I do not even speak of the educational implications of such an approach – if there is an "explanation" or a pat "answer" for everything, what will you tell your child when he or she asks: "Why did the Shoah happen?"[97]

Rabbi Amital stands here in a completely different place than where he had stood for many years when he tried to find meaning in historical events. He notes that it is specifically the explanation for historical events that removes the Holocaust from one's religious consciousness, since one can give no explanation for the Holocaust. The Holocaust must remain in a place where it is given no explanation. The will to leave the Holocaust unexplained entails a religious and educational approach that maintains that all evil should be left without explanation. This, in turn, leads to the next step. Rabbi Amital, who places the Holocaust in such a central position in Jewish experience, and who regards it as inexplicable, arrives at a place where it is extremely difficult to provide a religious explanation for events at all. Removal of the Holocaust from the continuum of history crushes our understanding of the meaning of historical events in general.

The tension between Rabbi Amital's position that the Holocaust is inexplicable, and the general position that he himself adopted for many years, maintaining that we may identify the

---

97. "Confronting the Holocaust," pp. 46–47.

meaning of events and the wisdom of Divine Providence as revealed in history, is difficult to bridge. Rabbi Amital, as we have seen, has stood for several years holding both ends of this rope, unwilling to relinquish either of these two positions. Each position is problematic in terms of the other, but they may be reconciled with difficulty. One of the ways of maintaining both simultaneously is to regard the Holocaust as a phenomenon that is exceptional, qualitatively different from other historical events. It alone remains without explanation, while all other events are revealed and open to interpretation. But even if the two positions can, with difficulty, be reconciled, it seems that the great tension between them may explain the change in Rabbi Amital's position.

4. THE HOLOCAUST IN THE PROCESS OF REDEMPTION?

As hinted above, Rabbi Amital's attitude towards the religious significance of the State of Israel has also changed over the years. It seems that this change, too, came about due to the memory of the Holocaust, which did not loosen its grip on his consciousness. In a speech delivered in 1974, Rabbi Amital proposes a "redemptive Zionism:" "The time has come for Zionism to make way for Zionism of redemption in our consciousness as well."[98] He speaks in terms that echo the teachings of Rabbi Kook: the signs of redemption, the stages of redemption, the vision of redemption and the light of the messiah, hidden and revealed:

> If we know that we are living in the generation of redemption, this adds to our strength. Indeed, we are capable of bringing the complete redemption... We are living in a great age... No matter how much of this faith – that we find ourselves in the process of redemp-

98. *HaMa'alot MiMa'amakim*, p. 43. In this article Rabbi Amital points to the crisis of Herzlian Religious Zionism, which speaks of solving the Jewish problem through the normalization of Jewish existence.

tion – is hidden, nevertheless it obligates us… The redemption is taking place ever so slowly before our eyes,
and this obligates us. Therefore we must emphasize and
make mention of the messiah continuously.[99]

Rabbi Amital held this position for many years. Thus, for example, in 1960 he declared that he accepted Rabbi Kook's authoritative opinion (*da'at Torah* [!]) concerning redemption, according to
which "the End has started, the third return has begun,"[100] despite
the great perplexity concerning the secularity of the State. The answers and solutions proposed by Rabbi Kook on this issue satisfied
him.[101]

It seems that for several years now, Rabbi Amital has become
increasingly reserved when it comes to interpretation of historical
events, including the religious significance of the State of Israel in
the process of redemption. The certainty with which he spoke in
his work *HaMa'alot MiMa'amakim,* containing discourses that were
delivered, for the most part, after the Yom Kippur War, has made
way for more reserved statements. The "redemption" philosophy has
been exchanged for a Religious Zionism that avoids using unequivocal terms of redemption in describing the State of Israel.[102]

This change finds expression on several levels. Firstly, Rabbi
Amital has, in recent years, begun again to speak of the State of Israel

99. Ibid., p. 75.
100. Ibid., p. 113, and the article as a whole.
101. The literature on this subject is extensive. Note particularly Ravitzky's
Messianism, especially chapter 3.
102. See below. The scope of this work does not allow for a classification of the
various streams of Religious Zionism. "Simple Zionism" and a "haven for
individuals" describe the type of Zionism proposed by Rabbi Reines. See:
E. Luz, *Parallels Meet*, Philadelphia 1988, chapter 9; Nehorai; Bat-Yehudah,
esp. pp. 79–90; Ravitzky, *Messianism*, especially chapter 3, and "Zionism and
Messianism in Orthodox Judaism – Historical and Conceptual Introduction"
in M. Kahana (ed.), *In the Throes of Tradition and Change*, Rehovot 1990, esp.
p. 225 onwards [Hebrew]. D. Schwartz has re-examined Rabbi Reines's position on this issue; see Schwartz's *Faith*, p. 67 onwards and esp. p. 73.

in terms of a home and refuge. He speaks of simple salvation, the type discussed by Rabbi Reines, the founder of Mizrahi. The change in his position is not declared openly; it appears quite innocently through an examination of his discourses on Israeli Independence Day from the middle of the 1980s onwards. His statements concerning redemption and the messiah are to be found no more. To the degree that the redemptive aspect of the State is weakened, the significance of the State as a home and place of refuge becomes stronger.

We find a more direct approach to this issue at the start of the 1990's. His statements are still not unequivocal, and his position in this regard is still hesitant and unclear. In the discourse for Independence Day 1993, Rabbi Amital hints that it is difficult to reconcile the Holocaust with the belief of leading Jewish authorities of the 19th and 20th century that we are living in the period of the "beginning of the redemption:"

> We cannot insert the establishment of the State of Israel into any verse in the Bible except for those that speak of the return to Zion. In the beginning of the redemption, there is no promise that "all will be okay." The students of the Vilna Gaon spoke of the "beginning of the redemption." Rabbi Eliyahu Guttmacher spoke of the "beginning of the redemption." Our teacher, Rabbi Kook, spoke of the "beginning of the redemption." And after all that came the Holocaust.[103]

Rabbi Amital notes the fact that in the midst of the period that the leading authorities of the Jewish nation characterized as the period of redemption, "came the Holocaust." Despite this, at the same time, Rabbi Amital still accepts the identification of the State of Israel as the "beginning of the redemption." He still desists from

---

103. "Guardian of Israel," p. 52.

stating explicitly that the Holocaust shattered and overturned the perception of the period as "the beginning of the redemption:"

> But the return to Zion continues and develops. We have no assurance that everything will go smoothly, but the process as a whole will lead towards the complete redemption; so we are promised.[104]

In this discourse, Rabbi Amital addresses the survival of the Jewish State, which is one of the "tests" in defining the State of Israel as the beginning of the redemption:

> After forty years of the State's existence, we still face great dangers. But I have full faith and belief that we shall overcome them. We remember the words of Rabbi Herzog, of blessed memory, when the Nazis were approaching the Land of Israel: "We have a tradition that there will be no third destruction."[105]

In the same discourse, though, Rabbi Amital expressed publicly his doubts as to the guaranteed survival of the State of Israel, and this appears to be the only time he has ever done so:

> Concerning one thing we are not certain, and I have to say this openly. We are promised that the nations of the world will not be able to destroy the State of Israel, but we are not certain that, God forbid, Jews themselves will not bring about her destruction. The possibility exists...[106]

---

104. Ibid.
105. Ibid.
106. Ibid. This was uttered against the backdrop of the sharp political debate surrounding the Oslo Accords. Further on in the discourse, Rabbi Amital denounces extreme movements on both sides of the political map, declar-

The significance of such a statement is a renewed appraisal of the ideology of the "beginning of the redemption." A more direct treatment of this ideology appears in a newspaper interview from the summer of the same year (1993).[107] Rabbi Amital responds to the position, espoused widely among Religious Zionists, that one's attitude towards the political situation may be based on the certainty that we are living in the midst of the process of redemption. Rabbi Amital explains his (new) attitude towards the question of the "beginning of the redemption" in terms of the Holocaust, which exploded the possibility of this explanation. Thus, it is specifically the Holocaust that obligates us to regard our present period as a "normal" one, rather than as a period of redemption. Such an attitude redefines the Religious Zionist viewpoint:

> What, in fact, was the innovation of Religious Zionism? It came and declared that there is a slow and gradual process of redemption, a natural process of entering history with all that that involves... They [the Haredim] rely on miracles. Religious Zionism, in contrast, maintains that we must assume responsibility, that we must act through natural means to ensure the well-being of the Jews and of the State.[108]

Rabbi Amital characterizes Religious Zionism as a world-view that does not rely on miracles, believing instead in a return to normality. He juxtaposes this with the ideology that perceives the State of Israel as the "beginning of the blossoming of our redemption" –

---

ing: "Gentlemen, if we do not watch ourselves we may come, God forbid, to destroying the State... A decision by a government elected by a democratic majority must be respected. One who treats it as something invalid nullifies, God forbid, Jewish sovereignty" (ibid.).

107. S. Schiff, "Earlier Generations Also Spoke of the 'Beginning of the Flowering of Our Redemption,' But After That Came the Holocaust," *HaTzofeh* August 13, 1993, Shabbat Supplement, p. 4.

108. Ibid. Rabbi Amital enlists the Haredi ideology in order to sharpen the self-definition of Religious Zionism.

an ideology relying on a political program that assumes success in advance, since we are living in the "beginning of the redemption," and is content with its faith that the Holy One will guard us in a supernatural way. Rabbi Amital rules that one who adopts this path is adopting something that is not Religious Zionism:

> ...It is in complete contradiction to the Religious Zionist world-view. The same applies when people speak of a Divine plan. This issue of the "beginning of the redemption" did not begin with the establishment of the State. The Vilna Gaon, the disciples of the Ba'al Shem Tov, and Rabbi Kook all dealt with it... and behold, despite this entire forecast, we were witness to the Holocaust... Thus we may say that we still have the obligation, so long as we do not have a prophet, to take steps as though we are at the beginning of the redemption, and to develop them in a natural way.[109]

So long as there is no prophecy, it is impossible to speak with certainty of the beginning of the redemption. The definition of the age as such is speculative, and it is impossible to base any kind of practical program on this assumption. This claim joins together with the claim that the estimation by the sages of Israel that they were living at the beginning of the redemption was demolished, since there cannot be a Holocaust in the midst of the process of redemption. The Holocaust testifies that our era is not one of redemption.

At the same time, in an article published in 1993, Rabbi Amital continues to deliberate publicly concerning these issues:

109. Ibid. Here Rabbi Amital touches upon the proximity of the Haredi starting point and the "redemptive" Zionist starting point. Concerning the proximity between positions that speak of a deterministic "beginning of the redemption" and Haredi positions maintaining that the future redemption will be deterministic – such as the position of Satmar Hassidim – see Ravitzky, *Messianism*. Faith in a deterministic "beginning of the redemption" is defined by Rabbi Amital as "relying upon miracles" – a reliance that exists in both camps.

The debate focused on two approaches in understanding the concept of the "beginning of the blossoming our redemption." There are those who claim that since this is a Divine process of redemption, then despite the fact that it is slow and gradual, the results are determined in advance – not only in relation to the end of the process, but also that success is guaranteed at each and every step of the way. Based on this view, there is no obligation to take the actual situation into account, the possible dangers, the political, social and economic situation, and the delays that may occur along the way. After all, it is an inexorable Divine process, independent of the nation's response to the Divine demands that are stated explicitly in the Torah.

In contrast with this view, there is another, according to which the only thing that is promised is the end of the process, while its duration, long or short, depends on our actions and our behavior. Since the process is natural and real, we have no guarantee that we will be met with success at each and every stage. Successes and failures are dependent on natural factors, on actions and failures for which the elected leadership of the nation are held responsible…[110]

In this article, Rabbi Amital still believes that we are in the midst of a redemptive process, as perceived by wide circles within the Religious Zionist public, who view the State of the Israel as the "beginning of the blossoming of our redemption." In their view, the process is deterministic and irreversible, and the assumption that we are living in the period of the third redemption is certain. Rabbi Amital accepts this view in principle. He agrees that the process leads towards redemption, but the duration of the process and its ups and downs are dependent on human behavior. Some two months

110. "Addressing the Challenges of a New Reality," p. 44.

after the appearance of this article, Rabbi Amital again raised the possibility that the greatest of the Religious Zionist thinkers had been mistaken:

> It is possible that all those who spoke of the "beginning of the blossoming of our redemption" were mistaken... Rabbi Akiva, the greatest of the *Tannaim*, was also mistaken. But there is one person concerning whom I cannot say that he was mistaken – that is the prophet[111]... A prophet does not make mistakes. But nevertheless, there is a great discrepancy between the reality of the Second Temple and the prophecy of Zachariah... A person who thinks that the prophecy of a prophet is not dependent on the spiritual behavior of the Children of Israel does not understand what prophecy is.[112]

Rabbi Amital speaks here of the possibility of error in interpreting the historical reality as one of redemption. It is possible that all those who spoke of "the beginning of the blossoming of our redemption" were mistaken, just as Rabbi Akiva was mistaken when he declared that Bar Kokhba "has the status of the King Messiah."[113] Moreover, even if there was no mistake, and we really are in a process of redemption, the redemption is not deterministic. It is dependent on the religious behavior of those who are being redeemed.[114] Note that Rabbi Amital here indeed speaks of redemption, but its path, character and duration depend on the conduct and worthiness of those being redeemed.[115] Accordingly, further on in the same article

111. Here Rabbi Amital quotes the prophecy of Zachariah, and speaks of the discrepancy between the prophecy and the reality of the Second Temple.
112. "Cry of an Infant," p. 85.
113. Jerusalem Talmud, *Ta'anit* 4:5.
114. This is similar to the position of Rabbi Soloveitchik in A. Ravitzky's schematic presentation.
115. Elsewhere Rabbi Amital attributes the nature and duration of the redemption process not to spiritual behavior alone, but also to our actual handling of the situation : "Addressing the Challenge of a New Reality."

he writes: "I continue to be a Zionist in heart and soul, and continue to believe in the 'beginning of the blossoming of our redemption' despite all of this."[116] The need for such a statement itself testifies to the fact that such faith is no longer a simple matter.

Rabbi Amital, who in the past accepted absolutely the analysis of Rabbi Kook, according to which we find ourselves in a progressive process of redemption, is now hesitant. Even if he repeats over and over that the State of Israel represents a "messianic phenomenon,"[117] he is not prepared to accept the historical interpretation of the school of Rabbi Kook, which perceives a continuum of redemption starting from the day that Jewish agricultural settlement of *Eretz Yisrael* began, and the land responded to the Jews who had returned to her. All of this was prior to the Second World War, and the expectation was that the process would progress towards the complete redemption. The Holocaust broke this continuum of progress. The impact of the Holocaust on the formulation of a Religious Zionist ideological position regarding the State of Israel becomes sharper:

> In 1996, I was asked to participate in a panel discussion. At one point, one of the participants asked me: "Is it still possible to refer to the State of Israel as 'the dawn of our redemption' now, after four cities were given over to the Palestinians as part of the Oslo Accords?" Immediately, a rabbi, one of the leaders of the Religious Zionist camp, stood up and replied, "It is an *a fortiori* argument: if, seventy years ago, Rabbi Kook in his correspondence could refer to the embryonic State of Israel as 'the dawn of our redemption,' certainly we can, all the more so, do likewise today!"
>
> Yet, in my mind, a question remained: "All the more so?" Is that really true? Was not our world de-

---

116. "Cry of an Infant," p. 86.
117. "Discourse for Independence Day [1998]," *Daf Kesher* vol. 7, p. 241 [Hebrew]; archived at http://www.etzion.org.il/dk/1to899/652daf.htm.

stroyed in the intervening seventy years? Did the most terrifying event not happen in the meantime?[118]

The world was destroyed. Now it is more difficult to speak of "the beginning of the blossoming of our redemption."

Rabbi Kook did not witness the Second World War, which made the First World War seem like child's play. He did not see Hiroshima and he did not see the terrible Holocaust...

We are wiser than Rabbi Kook. We saw the Second World War and the Holocaust. He never had a dilemma – the only possibility that faced him was that of the beginning of the great redemption.[119]

It is difficult to maintain that the State of Israel is the "foundation of God's throne in the world;"[120] it is difficult to regard the internal moral reality as one in which the vision of Rabbi Kook is being realized:

> The Rabbi [Kook] believed that there is apparently something in the innermost essence of the nation. Perhaps the option of achieving that great vision – the messianic world vision – was opened. Ultimately, the heretics of his day were not the same sort of heretics that once existed. They were not materialistic; they were selfless. They abandoned the Torah because they were not satisfied by it, not out of careerism. At the same time,

118. "Confronting the Holocaust," p. 47. The discourse was delivered in July 1998.

119. Transcript of discourse from Hannukah 1996, pp. 5–6. Certain sections were omitted from the printed version ("Religious Significance"). It is instructive to note that Hiroshima is also perceived by Rabbi Amital as having broken the continuity of the redemptive process.

120. RAYH Kook, *Orot Yisrael*, p. 160.

the Rabbi spoke very cautiously about the great thing that was going to take place in *Eretz Yisrael*...

We do not think that our current generation, with all its careerism and materialism, is capable of building that world vision about which the Rabbi would speak – ... "The State of Israel [is] the foundation of God's throne in the world; its entire aim is that God should be One and His Name One."[121] To apply this definition, this concept, to the State of Israel of our times is a distortion...[122]

Rabbi Amital does not shy away from bringing concrete examples taken from the social reality of the State of Israel at the end of the 1990's as well – crime, violence, corruption and social gaps.[123] Below we shall see that his sensitivity and sense of moral mission, together with the demand for the sanctification of God's Name through moral example, were also sharpened by the Holocaust.

Yet still Rabbi Amital states explicitly that the State of Israel is a "messianic phenomenon." But the source of this belief lies elsewhere. In order to understand the religious significance of the State, Rabbi Amital suggests a model that is taken from Jewish historical memory as described by Maimonides, and from the religious and moral world-view that accompany this memory.[124]

5. RABBI AMITAL VS. RABBI ZVI YEHUDAH KOOK AND HIS DISCIPLES

Rabbi Amital sees himself as a student of Rabbi Kook. He testifies to the profound closeness that he feels to his writings: "My entire world-view is influenced by our teacher, Rabbi Kook, of blessed

121. Ibid.
122. Transcript of discourse from Hannukah 1996, pp 5–6.
123. "Religious Significance," p. 140.
124. See Appendix A, below.

memory. Everything within me that is good – I received from his writings."[125] Rabbi Amital likewise attributes his political world-view to the influence of Rabbi Kook's writings.[126] Even his definition of reality as not matching Rabbi Kook's vision is based on statements of Rabbi Kook himself, who believed and expected that the return of the Jewish nation to world politics would bring about the creation of a State that was pure both socially and morally, both inwardly and outwardly.

This relationship can also be traced back to the place that Rabbi Kook's writings held in Rabbi Amital's heart in the dark days of his incarceration in a Nazi labor camp:

> I became aware of the writings of the Rabbi [Kook] at quite an early age, while still in Hungary, where I was born. As a young yeshivah student, I was studying a book about legends of our Sages, by a modern author, and I came upon a quote, an excerpt from [Rabbi Kook's] *Orot*. It was night, and I saw that there was a great light. It seized my imagination. I began to search for writings by the Rabbi...
>
> I was seventeen when the Germans came, and I was summoned to be transported to a labor camp in an unknown location – the Siberian plains or the Carpathian mountains. I had to take leave from my parents, and our feeling was that this was to be a final farewell (for what had happened to our Jewish brethren in Poland was no secret to us). I didn't know what awaited me. I took a few small books in a bag: a Pentateuch, Prophets, Mishnah, and I thought there would be a need for something else, that would perhaps maintain the necessary morale in hard times. And so I

125. Transcript of discourse for Hannukah 1996, p. 2.
126. Ibid.

took *Mishnat HaRav*[127] as well. Indeed, I received encouragement and strength from that book. The ideas and words influenced me to such a degree that I attributed to them my steadfast endurance in the labor camp, not contaminating myself with forbidden foods even when this involved great hunger, etc...[128]

The fact that his entire world-view is influenced by Rabbi Kook does not entail an insistence that all of Rabbi Kook's teachings are relevant to our generation (and in this sense, Rabbi Amital differs from numerous other disciples of Rabbi Kook's teachings):

The Rabbi [Kook] did not foresee – nor was he capable of foreseeing – either the Holocaust or its consequences. Therefore he read the map of reality the way he read it, and some of his statements have become irrelevant. The stubbornness in regarding everything that he wrote and said as relevant, as though nothing has happened, has caused us to miss messages in his teachings that are important for us specifically in our generation.[129]

Although everything that I teach is from Rabbi Kook, that does not mean that I agree completely with Rabbi Zvi Yehudah Kook, of blessed memory. I believe that he went on his own path – and this was his greatness... The path of Rabbi Zvi Yehudah Kook is different from my own.[130]

Rabbi Amital claims that there exists an interpretation of

---

127. This work is a collection of Rabbi Kook's ideas compiled by Rabbi Moshe Zvi Neriah.
128. Rabbi A.Y. Kook, *Mishnat HaRav*, Rabbi M.Z. Neriah (ed.), 3rd edition, Beit El 1992, pp. 147–148 [Hebrew].
129. Transcript of discourse for Hannukah 1996, p. 2.
130. Ibid., p. 3.

Rabbi Kook that is different from that of Rabbi Zvi Yehudah, and it arises from the principles of Rabbi Kook himself.[131] The necessity of finding a different interpretation of Rabbi Kook's writings – and even the ability to claim that he was mistaken – arise from the Holocaust, whose horrors took place after Rabbi Kook's death. It should be remembered that the analysis of the ways of God in history is itself attributed by Rabbi Amital to the school of Rabbi A.Y. Kook. This mode of analysis was shattered in the face of the Holocaust, after which there is nothing but muteness.

The school of Rabbi Zvi Yehudah Kook, which also claims to follow the path of Rabbi A.Y. Kook, adopts a different view. It was the school of Rabbi Zvi Yehudah that generated the harsh theological statement that God Himself brought on the Holocaust as a kind of surgery, "a heavenly surgery, performed through the hands of the destroyers, may their memory be erased."[132] This harsh statement was passed down in different formulations by his students, and echoes of it may be found in Religious Zionist ideology and its attitude towards the State of Israel. The starting point for this position is a view of Divine immanence in creation, which – as noted above – is the cultural climate in which Religious Zionism exists. Such a picture of the world pushes one who has completely internalized it into this severe position concerning the Holocaust. Aviezer Ravitzky recently addressed the connection between the philosophy of immanence and this stance:

131. "My ability to assert that some of Rabbi Kook's teachings are not relevant… I received from Rabbi Kook, of blessed memory" (ibid., p. 2). Rabbi Amital makes a comment that hints at the responses to his positions among many in the Religious Zionist camp. He states that one of the things he learned from Rabbi Kook was "the ability to stand alone, sometimes against an entire congregation" (ibid.). This feeling arises explicitly or implicitly in other places, too. See, for example, *Alon Shevut Bogrim* 9, 1996, p. 178. The scope of this work does not allow for further elaboration.

132. RZYH Kook, *Discourses – Tazria, Metzora, Yom haShoah*, p. 11. See also Rabbi David Samson, *Torat Eretz Yisrael: The Teachings of HaRav Tzvi Yehuda HaCohen Kook*, Jerusalem 1991, chapter 10 (The Holocaust).

Consider: If a believer maintains a transcendent view of God, he is likely to speak of "hiding of the face" and a catastrophic "eclipse of the light," of a God who temporarily distanced Himself from the nation, from man, from history. But this possibility is closed to a pantheist. His God is meant to be available to him here and now, within the historical cosmic system and not outside of it. It is therefore no wonder that the Lubavitcher Rebbe, Rabbi M.M. Schneerson, on the one hand, and Rabbi Zvi Yehudah Kook, on the other hand, are two modern sages who explain the Holocaust as a process of healing, as a Divine "surgery" and "treatment" performed on the body of the nation in preparation for its redemption.[133]

Rabbi Zvi Yehudah Kook speaks of the Holocaust as an operation of amputation from exile. He relates to the nation of Israel as a single body:

We are all one nation, one whole body, one national and public body. And now it is necessary to remove all of Israel from the exile, and it is necessary to cut and to perform surgery on the body of the nation.[134]

Such an approach ignores the individual, and from here the path to speaking of "surgery" is short:

"And I took you out from the nations... with a strong hand... and with an outpouring of anger" (Ezekiel 20:34): The nation of Israel was taken, cut from the depths of exile to the State of Israel. The spilling of the blood of six million was a real incision into the

133. A. Ravitzky, *Freedom*, pp. 109–110.
134. RZYH Kook, *Discourses – Tazria, Metzora, Yom haShoah*, p. 10.

national body… The body public of the Jewish People must be yanked away and severed from everything that surrounds it. The entire nation underwent a heavenly surgery performed through the hands of the destroyers, may their name be blotted out, through the impurity of Amalek. This operation is very painful, terrible and terrifying, painful. The nation has been cut.[135]

According to Rabbi Zvi Yehudah Kook, there is a reason for this surgery – the need to sever the nation from the exile:

The nation of God was so entangled in the impurity of the land of the gentiles that it needed to be cut and separated from it with a cost in lives when the time for the End (redemption) came.[136]

Out of the cruel surgery… the essence of our lives is revealed, the rebirth of the nation and the rebirth of the land… Through the Divine treatment, God's glory returns to God's nation, to God's land. One must see this comprehensive Divine historical, cosmological fact. Seeing means more than understanding: seeing means encounter, an encounter with the Master of the Universe.[137]

---

135. Ibid., p. 11.
136. Ibid. A similar message was delivered in a previous discourse of Rabbi Zvi Yehudah on the Holocaust. There he explains at length the need for this surgery: "When the time for redemption arrives, it may happen that there are complications, and a large portion of the Jewish People are stuck to the exile. And so it was: many Jews have become accustomed to the impurity of exile and refuse to leave it. Even some of the truly righteous are sometimes connected to exile and its impurity. And so begins an internal, deep and hidden Divine process of purification from this impurity, surgery and healing" (RZYH Kook, *Discourses – Aharei Mot, Counting of the Omer, The Holocaust, Kedoshim, Emor*, pp. 15–16).
137. RZYH Kook, *Discourses – Tazria, Metzora, Yom haShoah*, p. 11.

Elsewhere Rabbi Zvi Yehudah explains that the meaning of events that happened to individuals is God's secret. This hints at the corollary: events that happen to the nation as a whole are revealed, known and open to explanation.[138]

Rabbi Zvi Yehudah Kook maintains that we are capable – even obligated – to understand "God's revelation in the world in all spheres: the revelation of God in nature and, no less than this, the revelation of God in history."[139] He maintains that we are able to understand even God's revelation in Europe of 1939–1945. Despite the reservation that mentions a Divine secret to which we are not party, Rabbi Zvi Yehudah reveals – in his view – the secret, as part of his discussion of the historical rupture of the Holocaust and the national revival, and their interpretation. The causal connection between the Holocaust and the national revival is explicit. The Holocaust is the "surgery" that facilitated the revival.

The same idea has been repeated by Rabbi Zvi Yehudah's disciple, Rabbi Shlomo Aviner,[140] who reiterates, explains and simplifies these points:

And the Master of the Universe is the address.[141]
Only of this can we be sure and certain – that He was there, that God performed all of this.[142]

---

138. RZYH Kook, Discourses – *Aharei Mot, Counting of the Omer, The Holocaust, Kedoshim, Emor*, p. 16.
139. Ibid., p. 11. I have discussed this approach at length above.
140. Aviner, "Holocaust;" *Waves*. Rabbi Aviner edited the discourses of Rabbi Zvi Yehudah and elaborates on them in his notes, inter alia by quoting great religious authorities who lived prior to the Holocaust (see: RZYH Kook, *Discourses – Aharei Mot, Counting of the Omer, The Holocaust, Kedoshim, Emor*, p. 16, note 29). Similar remarks are to be found in Aviner, "Holocaust," p. 59 ff.
141. Aviner, "Holocaust," p. 54.
142. Aviner, *Waves*, p. 39.

Rather, we are forced to say, as difficult as this may be: God wanted the Holocaust to happen! Had He not wanted it, He would not have let it happen.[143]

It is a fact that the nation of Israel was very attached to the exile, both in body and in spirit. And it is possible that surgery was needed in order to sever it... We do not mean to say that this was a punishment for cleaving to the exile. It is very difficult for our humble lips to discuss such things... Rather, we mean that this was a Divine treatment, a cruel Divine surgery, which severed the nation from the impurity of exile. That is a fact.[144]

To see the Holocaust as a punishment is difficult for Rabbi Aviner.[145] It is easier for him to see it as a deliberate Divine act in preparation for the redemption. These ideas are stated over and over by the disciples of Rabbi Zvi Yehudah and their circles of students.[146]

Rabbi Amital rejects this position outright. In his eyes, it is a desecration of God's Name. He rejects both the ideological position that the Holocaust and the national revival are connected, as well as its theological explanation:

In the past, very grave opinions were expounded regarding the Holocaust: there were those who claimed that the Holocaust was a sort of price that the Jewish People had to pay in order that the Jewish State could be established. There are those who claimed that the State

---

143. Ibid., p. 285.
144. Aviner, "Holocaust," p. 59.
145. "We cannot say that the reason was a punishment, for the explanation of punishment is disproportionate" (Aviner, *Waves*, p. 288).
146. For instance: Aviner, "Holocaust," p. 51, note 1; D. Shneur, *Paths of Light* (Discourses of Rabbi Haim Druckman), Jerusalem 1991, p. 94 [Hebrew]; Rabbi Y. Hess, *Faith for the Generation of Rebirth*, Jerusalem 1990, pp. 169–233 [Hebrew].

of Israel is the divine compensation for the destruction of the Holocaust. There were even those who claimed that the Shoah was the only way – or, at least in practical terms, became the impetus – to compel the Jews of Europe to immigrate to the Land of Israel. These are very difficult claims, approaches that I find hard to countenance at all.[147]

In an ideological framework such as that presented by Rabbi Zvi Yehudah and his followers, only an absolute, comprehensive answer can balance the loss and demonic destruction of the Holocaust. Such an answer requires the elevation and sanctification of the State of Israel.[148] Faced with such an answer, Rabbi Amital declared in a discourse delivered in 1990:

> No worldly attainment can compensate for the murder of those millions. All the claims about the establishment of the State of Israel serving as compensation for the Holocaust are hollow. Neither the State of Israel that exists in reality, that fights bloody wars for its existence from time to time, nor the ideal State of Israel, as in the vision of "Every man under his vine and under his fig tree" (Micah 4:4), can justify even partially what the nation of Israel went through during the Holocaust years.[149]

Rabbi Amital strongly rejects any causal connection between the Holocaust and the State. In recent years he has even – for various reasons and from various perspectives – rejected identifying the

---

147. "Confronting the Holocaust," pp. 47–48. One cannot help but note the connection between the rejection of Rabbi Zvi Yehudah's approach to the Holocaust and the fact that Rabbi Amital does not adopt the immanent view.
148. In the estimation of Ravitzky, *Messianism*, 126–128.
149. "A Kaddish," p. 7.

contemporary reality of the State of Israel with the reality of an ideal State. The Holocaust was a terrible experience "in the final stages of the exile and before the redemption,"[150] devoid of any connection to either the end of the exile or to the beginning of the redemption.

6. THE HOLOCAUST AND THE
ESTABLISHMENT OF THE STATE

The Holocaust and the establishment of the State occurred in close chronological proximity. "Both denote and symbolize the existential catastrophe and the national watershed that not only transformed the Jews' destiny but also affected their image as a people by furnishing them with a fundamental myth (*Grundungsmythos*) that explains their collective existence."[151] The sense of mystery that arises from the astounding proximity of these two events has nurtured theological, historical, public and ideological debate in Israel. "The 'Holocaust and national revival' (*Shoah u-tekumah*) juxtaposition has become, over the course of time – at least in the State of Israel – a permanent combination,"[152] as part of the ideological, public and national debate, and has even had a considerable influence on academic-historical research, which is meant at least to create a chronological historical framework.[153]

Often, Rabbi Amital discusses these two chronologically

---

150. Ibid.
151. Gorni, p. 221.
152. Michman, "Connection," p. 60.
153. On the possibility or impossibility of a causal-historical connection between the Holocaust and the establishment of the State of Israel in the view of Israeli scholars, see: Y. Bauer, "The Holocaust and the Battle of the Yishuv as a Factor in the Establishment of the State," *Holocaust and Revival*, Jerusalem 1978, pp. 31–34, 67–91 [Hebrew]; A. Prizel, "The Destruction of European Jewry – a Factor in the Establishment of the State of Israel?," *Molad* 39–40 (249–250), vol. 8 (31), 1980, pp. 21–32 [Hebrew]; Michman, "Connection," p. 60 onwards; Gorni. For a broad review of this subject, see: D. Michman, "From Holocaust to Revival: Historiography of the Causal Connection Between the Holocaust and the Establishment of the State of Israel," *Studies in the Revival of Israel* 10, 2000, p. 234 ff [Hebrew].

juxtaposed events – the Holocaust and the establishment of the State of Israel – and the meaning of their proximity. The mystery of the juxtaposition of two such complete opposites creates a theological temptation to provide some explanation. Rabbi Amital vehemently rejects any explanation of the Holocaust as part of a messianic process leading ultimately to the redemption. He does point to the establishment of the State as a miracle whose magnitude is highlighted against the backdrop of the chronologically proximate Holocaust. But even if the establishment of the State is somewhat of a healing for the survivors, or somewhat of a healing for the desecration of God's Name caused by the Holocaust, he will not agree to see any causal relationship (either historical or theological) between the Holocaust and the establishment of the State of Israel. Such a connection is precluded by his essence, by his religious and ethical perspective.

Placing the establishment of the State and the Holocaust in the same context creates a symmetry between the establishment of the State and the Holocaust. Rabbi Amital, who regards the establishment of the State as a miracle, is not prepared to create such a symmetry. It is for this reason that he rejects outright and unequivocally any historical causal connection leading from the Holocaust to the State of Israel. He likewise rejects strongly any theological causal connection between them. We have noted above that Rabbi Amital claims that attempts to draw a connection between the Holocaust and the establishment of the State are "very difficult claims, approaches that I find hard to countenance at all,"[154] and that there is nothing in the world – including the State of Israel – that can serve as compensation for the Holocaust.[155] Rabbi Amital comes back again and again to this vigorous rejection:

> The establishment of the State of Israel does not explain why millions of Jews were led to their deaths. I do not

---

154. "Confronting the Holocaust," p. 48.
155. "A Kaddish," p. 7.

accept the theory that has since been espoused by many, that the State of Israel gives reason and answer to the Holocaust.[156]

To see the State of Israel as compensation for the Holocaust, as though this suffering were required for the establishment of the State – I cannot imagine this.[157]

Any such statements about the establishment of the State in the wake of the Holocaust, are hollow statements. Neither the State of Israel in reality – which must shed its blood from time to time to maintain its very existence – nor the ideal State of Israel, with its vision of "each man under his vine and under his fig-tree" (Micah 4:4), can justify in any measure what happened to the nation of Israel during the Holocaust years.[158]

Rabbi Amital objects to those who speak of the suffering and

156. "Forty Years Later," p. 88.
157. "A World Built," p. 14. Prior to this Rabbi Amital comments: "These are certainly the birth-pangs of the Messiah" (ibid., p. 13). His words are obscure, for he rejects a causal connection between the establishment of the State and the redemption, and a sentence such as this explicitly presents the Holocaust as "birth-pangs of the Messiah." Is it possible to sever the "birth-pangs of the Messiah" from the "redemption," claiming that there is no connection between them? "The birth-pangs of Messiah" is a concept drawn from the Jewish traditions of redemption. Rabbi Amital's explanation for his opposition to any connection between the redemption and the "birth-pangs of the Messiah," as presented here, arises from his internal sense of morality. The nullification of the causal connection between them is possible, for the birth-pangs of the Messiah are not a necessary precondition to the arrival of redemption. See *Sanhedrin* 98b, which discusses the possibility of being saved from these "birth-pangs." See also *Mekhilta de-Rabbi Yishma'el, Vayisa, parasha* 4, Horowitz-Rabin edition, p. 169 [Hebrew], and in parallel texts. See also Urbach, p. 671 note 67 and note 68, and the discussion as a whole, pp. 668–673. See, in contrast, Aviner, "Holocaust," pp. 57–58. Rabbi Aviner quotes from rabbinic sources on this subject. See also Gershom Scholem, *Devarim be-Go*, Tel Aviv 1975, p. 155–190 [Hebrew].
158. "A World Built," p. 7. Recently: Rabbi Y. Amital, "The Last Shore," *Meimad*

sacrifice as having been meant to give rise to the salvation and re-demption:

> Redemption is a great thing. It is not only the redemp-tion of Israel, but also the redemption of man, the redemption of the worlds, the redemption of human-kind... [and despite this, Rabbi Haim Vital told Rabbi Isaac Luria:] If the redemption of Israel is dependent on harm to others, I have no desire for it.[159]

7. "HE SETTLES INDIVIDUALS IN A HOME:" THE ESTABLISHMENT OF THE STATE AS SIMPLE REDEMPTION FOR INDIVIDUALS

In recent years, Rabbi Amital has again emphasized the role of the State of Israel as a healing for the Holocaust, as a shore of refuge, a home, a place where one may acquire freedom. This is not redemp-tion in the messianic sense, but rather redemption in the sense of a home – a simple salvation, the feeling of freedom of one who has seen city lights from afar, and knows that they do not shine for him. These, in essence, are the roles that Herzlian Zionism be-stowed on the yearned-for State. The possibility that Rabbi Amital is consciously following the example of Rabbi Reines here cannot be ruled out.[160] An echo of Rabbi Reines's words concerning "simple salvation" is to be found in a discourse delivered by Rabbi Amital on Independence Day 2000:

22, 2001; "To Hear the Groan of a Prisoner," *Daf Kesher* #810 (2001), http://www.etzion.org.il/dk/1to899/801daf.htm.

159. "A World Built," p. 14.

160. "But here this man comes to us bearing tidings of a simple salvation. He does not refer to the complete redemption, but only shows that there is a way to improve the lot of Israel and to raise their horn with honor, to attempt to seek a safe place of refuge" (Rabbi Y.Y. Reines, *A New Light Upon Zion*, New York 1946, p. 278 [Hebrew]). See also: Nehorai; Bat-Yehudah, especially pp. 79–90.

At the time of the establishment of the State, I was party – together with the entire nation – to the dream of the establishment of the State of the Jews: not necessarily a messianic State, in which all citizens would repent and return to religion, but a "simple" State, in accordance with the Herzlian vision.[161]

This is a policy statement concerning the essence and religious significance of the State of Israel. Rabbi Amital sees the State as a shore of refuge for wanderers and refugees who have been pushed from place to place:

We certainly see in the State of Israel a process of healing. I cannot imagine what would have happened to the Jewish People had it not been for the establishment of the State. How vital it was for the psychological rehabilitation of the survivors! When I picture the "survivors of the sword" – if these people had had to continue moving from one shore to the next, not finding a place of refuge in the Land of Israel, what would have happened to the Jewish People? From this point of view, there is certainly a connection.[162]

The State of Israel serves as a home for individuals, a solution to the tragedy of homeless refugees. Before speaking about the exile and redemption of the nation as a whole, we first have to perceive the suffering and the relief of the individual: hundreds of thousands of refugees who, as individuals, found their home. This theme repeats itself over and over in Rabbi Amital's discourses on Independence Day:

161. Rabbi Y. Amital, "The Great Sound of Celebration and the Sound of the Nation Crying," *Daf Kesher* vol. 8, p. 263 [Hebrew], archived at http://www.etzion.org.il/dk/1to899/759daf.htm.
162. "A World Built," p. 14.

[Psalm 68 teaches us that] in all the great servitude and the sufferings of Egypt, there were individuals with their own tragedies, homeless people. If a person who toils and suffers has a place that he leaves from and a small plot to which he returns at the end of a hard day, then his suffering is bearable. But there were individuals who lacked such a home. One cannot address the Exodus from Egypt before examining what was given to individuals...

I heard the proclamation of the State, but those were mere words. We sought the independence: where was it? How was it expressed? Even before the Sabbath began,[163] we heard that "He settles individuals in a home" (Psalms 68:7); hundreds of people, Holocaust refugees, had drifted at sea for months, seeking a home, a modest private domain, and there wasn't a single nation in the world willing to give them a home of even "four ells." They experienced a feeling of homelessness.

Indeed, the first expression of independence was, "He settles individuals in a home." There is nothing greater than a home... and not only for those individuals who came and found a home after years in concentrations camps and extermination camps.[164]

The sense of freedom and liberty cannot be clear to someone who had no personal experience of liberation. One's personal, autobiographical experience cannot be separated from the determination of the significance of the events. An understanding of the events is impossible without feeling total empathy with those who experienced the liberation:

163. The declaration of the State of Israel took place on a Friday (May 14, 1968).
164. Rabbi Y. Amital, "He Settles Individuals in a Home," *Daf Kesher* vol. 1, pp. 4–5 [Hebrew] (Independence Day 1985); archived at http://www.etzion. org.il/dk/1to899/002daf.htm.

I knew what liberation was. Sometimes I walk about in the city and touch, feel, the freedom… Sometimes it is difficult for me to rejoice in the public joy, for I rejoice in my own private joy for the fact that I am free… But you [young students], who never knew subjugation, … are you capable of listing the favors, sensing the freedom, that the Holy One has given us, feeling as though you came out of Egypt?[165]

There is a large public that was born in the State of Israel. Even those who were not born in the State of Israel were born in countries where there is freedom, countries where Jews walk freely, and therefore they are unable to understand the great profundity of God's blessing of Jewish sovereignty with the establishment of the State of Israel; it seems obvious to them. They seek [significance] in the miracles that took place on the fifth of Iyar in the War of Independence. But [the miracle of] independence itself – the very freedom of Israel – can be felt only by one who has lived in other conditions, conditions in which Jews did not have freedom, in which Jews did not dare walk freely in the streets; Jews lived in bunkers, longing for light – they looked from afar at the lights from the cities, but knew that they were not shining for them… The revival of Jewish sovereignty, the State of Israel, is a great thing that is not obvious, and first and foremost we have to thank the Holy One for the fact that Jews walk freely throughout the world.[166]

We can all identify with the simple significance of the establishment of Israel forty years ago. "A person is obligated to view himself as though he came out of Egypt" (Mishnah *Pesahim* 10:5). Thousands of people,

---

165. "Not By Their Sword," p. 47.
166. "This is the Day," pp. 13–14.

survivors of death-camps and extermination camps, drifted about in ships in the middle of the sea – a lone survivor of a town, two survivors of an entire family – attempting to enter Palestine, and the gates were locked. And on that day [of Israel's independence] the gates were opened. Survivors who had been through hell and remained in the camps were unable to return to the home of their forefathers. Freedom was still denied to them. And behold, the gates were opened. The day of liberation! This is sufficient reason for us to thank God.[167]

Despite the emphasis on the ramifications of the establishment of the State as pertaining to the individual, Rabbi Amital certainly does not ignore its broad national significance: Jewish sovereignty and Jewish national independence. The salvation of individuals cannot come about without Jewish sovereignty. In this we find a return to the Herzlian model of Zionism:

But we have to thank God not only for the past, but also for the "miracles and wonders that are at all times, evening and morning and noon" – for the fact that our sovereignty exists, for the fact that we have a government… A Jewish policeman – that says something to me. A Jewish soldier![168]

The same idea is expressed clearly in other places as well. There is no possibility of salvation without a Jewish State:

The blessing and thanks to the Holy One for the State of Israel are, first and foremost, a blessing for Jewish sovereignty. Forty-five years ago, Jews wandered about

167. "Not By Their Sword," p. 47.
168. Ibid.

the world with nothing. Holocaust refugees, dozens and thousands who remained in Germany after the Holocaust, were in camps… What would have happened to those Jews had the State of Israel not arisen?[169]

8. *HAMA'ALOT MIMA'AMAKIM* – THE STEPS FROM THE DEPTHS

We have seen above that Rabbi Amital rejects any causal connection between the Holocaust and the establishment of the State of Israel. At the same time, though, he comes back again and again to the lines leading from the Holocaust to the State. The chronological proximity of these two events emphasizes the miracle and the uniqueness of the establishment of the State of Israel. There is no connection, but one cannot ignore the proximity.

> My beard has still not turned white with age, and yet during the course of my life I have seen, as our Sages have said, "a world built, destroyed, and rebuilt." I have seen Jews being led to Auschwitz; I have seen Jews dance at the establishment of the State of Israel; I have seen the great victories of the Six-Day War; I have traveled with soldiers to the Suez Canal.[170]

And, in a much sharper form, Rabbi Amital said to soldiers in 1973:

> Jewish history in the past thirty years has been a period of great intensity. It started with Jews being led to gas chambers like sheep to the slaughter, and immediately

169. "Guardian of Israel," p. 52.
170. "Forty Years Later," pp. 88–89.

thereafter – the nation arose like a lion: the War of Independence, the Six Day War, the Yom Kippur War. Thirty years ago – absolute disregard for Jewish existence, and just a few years later – Israel at the center of the world. If the world were to be destroyed, Heaven forbid, in a nuclear holocaust, and historians of the future were to attempt to recreate the events of our times, they would discover archaeological artifacts testifying on the one hand to the Holocaust in Europe, and on the other hand to the State of Israel, its wars and its world status. There can be no doubt that they would conclude that these events took place in different eras, with a distance of hundreds of years between them. But in fact all this has happened to us in our generation, in the space of thirty years.[171]

It would seem that despite the rejection of any causal connection between the Holocaust and the establishment of the State, the proximity of these two events – both as historical fact and as existential experience – has created a link between them for Rabbi Amital. Firstly, it is a link created by virtue of the context. The very presentation of the miracle inherent in the establishment of the State against the backdrop of the Holocaust – even if this is done amidst an explicit rejection of any causal connection between them – leaves these two events within the same context. A different, admittedly weaker, link between the Holocaust and the establishment of the State is to be found in the fact that the State provided a home for individuals, and we have seen above that Rabbi Amital emphasizes this point over and over. This link also finds expression in Rabbi Amital's claim that the motivation to define the State of Israel as a State that fits into an irreversible process of redemption, arises from

---

171. *HaMa'alot MiMa'amakim*, pp. 37–38. See also ibid., pp. 21–22, and elsewhere.

the fact that it represents the sole healing for the scar left on the Jewish soul by the survival anxiety of the Holocaust:

> Dozens of years will pass before people will research and try to understand something of what happened in the recesses of the Jewish soul that remained after the Holocaust. How deep and great is the scar that the Holocaust left behind on the soul of Israel. If we had come after the Holocaust and said to the Jewish survivors that now there would be quiet, another episode of quiet among the nations, not another Holocaust but rather quiet – we can imagine what it would have led to. What would have happened to these Jews, had it not been for the faith that the reward so yearned for was indeed starting? If we view the events in their messianic dimension, they tell us that there is no turning back.[172]

A stronger link appears when Rabbi Amital speaks about how the existence of the State of Israel repairs the desecration of God's Name in the Holocaust.[173] He has mentioned this idea often, in general contexts – the establishment of the State is a sanctification of God's Name, just as the exile and the Holocaust were a desecration of His name:

> If we believe that the State of Israel represents a refuge for millions of Jews, may they increase... and if we believe that the revival of the State of Israel and its existence contains something of a sanctification of God's Name, as Rabbi Menahem Ziemba wrote – may God avenge his blood: "Those who wish to see soon the establishment of Jewish sovereignty – this is because of

---

172. Ibid., p. 74.
173. "Sing to Him," p. 55; transcript of discourse for Hannukah 1996, p. 7.

their great desire to sanctify the Name of Heaven in the
eyes of the nations, to show them that after thousands
of years, with the nation of Israel wandering and drift-
ing in the world, their hope is not lost, and they shall
still live."[174] This was said in the period prior to the
Holocaust, and it assumes special significance in the
period following it.[175]

For the opening of the gates of the Land of Israel
to immigration, for the great sanctification of God's
Name in the revival of the State of Israel, for "God desires His people, He shall glorify the humble with salvation" (Psalms 149:4).[176]

How can one not thank the Holy One on this
day? ... And [how much more so] if we add the tim-

---

174. Rabbi M. Ziemba, *Hiddushei Ha-Gaon Rabbi Menahem Ziemba*, Bnei Berak
1980, *siman* 54, p. 124 [Hebrew]. Rabbi Ziemba, a leading rabbinic scholar
in Poland, subsequently perished in the Warsaw Ghetto uprising.

175. Rabbi Y. Amital, "The Status of the Secular Jew in Our Days," in Rabbi Y.
Shaviv (ed.), *A Kingdom of Priests and a Holy Nation*, Jerusalem 1989, p. 343
[Hebrew].

176. "This is the Day," p. 14. We deduce from this that the demand for a sanctification of God's Name is addressed, as it were, to God Himself, too. A study
of the Bible demonstrates the source of this idea: "... And the nations who
have heard of Your fame will say, It was for lack of God's ability to bring this
nation to the land which He promised to them that He slaughtered them in
the wilderness" (Numbers 14:15–16). The disaster that befalls the children of
Israel will be interpreted by the nations as arising from God's incompetence,
as it were. This is a desecration of God's Name. Similarly, Ezekiel describes
the ingathering of the exiles and the renewal in the Land of Israel as an act
aimed to sanctify God's Name in the world: "It is not for your sakes that I do
this, O children of Israel, but rather for My holy name which you have desecrated among the nations where you went" (Ezekiel 36:22). In other words,
the exile itself is a desecration of God's Name, and there will be a sanctification of God's Name in the ingathering of the exiles and the spiritual renewal
that will follow it: "And I shall sanctify My great name, which was profaned
among the nations... and I shall take you from among the nations and gather
you up from all the lands and bring you to your land. And I shall sprinkle
pure water over you, and you shall be purified" (ibid., 23–25).

ing – that this happened after the terrible Holocaust that we went through, and the fact that this was the first time in the history of the nation of Israel after the exile that there was a sanctification of God's Name on such a huge scale, in contrast to the great desecration of God's Name in the exile itself and the destruction of the land, that for the first time the nation of Israel arose and demonstrated bravery from amidst the Holocaust and merited independence, the first time that the gates of *Eretz Yisrael* were opened wide.[177]

There is a link; nevertheless, it is a weak link, post facto, not a strong theological link like that of Rabbi Zvi Yehudah and his disciples – not even a more moderate link, describing a Divine plan that links the redemption with the birth-pangs of the Messiah that precede it. According to these views, the catastrophe is a precondition for redemption, whether in the form of "Divine surgery" or in the form of a preconceived Divine historical order. Rabbi Amital speaks of healing after the disaster: a personal healing for the suffering of individuals, and a healing for the desecration of God's Name that took place. Once the Holocaust already took place, there was a need for healing and repair. There is no historical causality here, only an attempt to relieve the terrible rupture.

177. "This is the Day," p. 15.

Chapter three

Basic Elements of Jewish Identity

I believe that in our times, the ABC of Jewish identity is identification with these two events: the Holocaust – in other words, Jewish fate – and the State of Israel, as the continuation of Jewish fate. Although there is no balance between these two events...

I say identification with the Holocaust: identification that is conscious; identification out of will; identification with the family of the murdered, and not with the murderers.

I think I have never recited the traditional blessing, "Who has not made me a gentile" – in other words, "Who has made me a Jew"[1] – with the same emotion as I did in the days when I saw myself amongst the family of the murdered, while on the other side the entire world

---

1. This is the positive formulation of the blessing; see S. Lieberman, *Tosefta ki-Fshutah, Berakhot*, Jerusalem 1993, p. 120 note 68 [Hebrew] and adjacent text. The formulation that appears in *Menahot* 43b is in the positive, while a different formulation appears in the manuscripts.

belonged to the family of the murderers – whether they were active murderers or people who stood silently by while children were killed. I believe that this must be demanded of every Jew, with Jewish pride. On the other hand, one must also see in the revival of Israel the unique Jewish fate, the continuation of the prophecy of "a nation that dwells alone" (Numbers 23:9), and I think that that is indeed a moral definition [of Jewish nationhood], but because of its morality, it does not seem harsh to me.[2]

I never said the blessing, "Blessed art Thou, Lord our God, King of the Universe, who did not make me a gentile," with such fervor, as I used to recite it during those dark days. Specifically during those days, especially during those days – despite everything, I was proud to be counted among the murdered and not the murderers.[3]

Rabbi Amital invests the blessing "Who has not made me a gentile" with new content and meaning:[4] It is the dividing line between the family of victims and the family of murderers. The use of the word "family" to connote group identity is not coincidental. The family is the primary source for identity definition. The fact of belonging to the family of victims is itself "Jewish pride." This is not pride in an active deed, not even an act of self-defense, but rather pride in something that the Israeli ethos denied, for many years, as a source of pride.[5]

2. "A World Built," pp. 12–13.
3. "Forty Years Later," p. 88.
4. See *Tosefta, Berakhot* 6:18. There is widespread rabbinical debate as to the proper understanding of these blessings. For a partial review, see: Rabbi Y. Yaakovson, *Netiv Binah*, 1, Tel Aviv 1964, pp. 89–90, 164 onwards [Hebrew].
5. See: Amos Funkenstein, *Perceptions of Jewish History*, Berkeley 1993; Anita Shapira, *Land and Power: The Zionist Resort to Force, 1881–1948*, New York 1992; see also in the collection: *Major Changes Within the Jewish People in*

In a lecture delivered on Holocaust Memorial Day, Rabbi Amital sharpened this point over and over. After speaking about the fact that the explanation and significance of the Holocaust were completely unintelligible to him, he claimed that there was one point that did have significance for our times, and that was the single clear meaning that we can learn from the Holocaust period:

> If there was a single point of light in the Holocaust, it was this: there were two camps there; on one side the camp of the murderers, and on the other side the camp of the murdered. Happy are we that we belonged to the camp of the murdered. The heavens and earth can testify on our behalf: if the nation of Israel had been given the opportunity to reverse roles, the nation of Israel would have said that it is preferable to be among the murdered than among the murderers. This is a historical point of light that cannot be overshadowed.[6]

Sensitivity to human life and fear of moral corruption are strengthened and sharpened by the memory of the Holocaust. What is generally perceived as a "universal message" of the Holocaust is considered by Rabbi Amital to be specifically its "Jewish message." In contrast to those who distinguish between the Jewish message of the Holocaust and its universal significance, Rabbi Amital identifies these two messages as a single one.[7] The internal obligation of moral behavior is what characterizes the Jewish national identity.

the Wake of the Holocaust, Jerusalem 1993, esp. the articles by A. Shapira, Y. Gelber and D. Shaked. This statement by Rabbi Amital was published already in 1977, at a time when such voices were barely a whisper in Israeli public debate.

6. "A Kaddish," p. 8.
7. Rabbi Amital states elsewhere that the messages emerging from the Holocaust are not the business of Jews only, but are rather of universal concern: "This was not a process that concerned only our nation. It was a universal process, an all-embracing dilemma. We must not consider only the individual, be-

2. MORAL FOUNDATIONS – CORNERSTONE
OF OUR CONCEPT OF NATIONALISM

a. "All the World on One Side, and He on the Other Side" [8]

In a discourse dealing with the demand for morality even in relation to the enemy, not out of halakhic obligation but rather out of internal moral conviction, Rabbi Amital stated:

> We are familiar with the nations of the world and their hypocrisy, we see now their denial of all that happened to Jews in the extermination camps... We owe them nothing. We owe it only to the Holy One, who entrusted us with a certain mission, to sanctify the Name of Heaven. [9]

This loss of faith in the nations of the world appears elsewhere, too, sometimes also in the context of the Holocaust. In a lecture after the Yom Kippur War, Rabbi Amital stated that the war had undermined some of the assumptions that had anchored the previously prevalent optimism. One of these assumptions was that "the countries committed to a heritage of human culture – whose conscience still troubles them over what happened to the Jews during the Holocaust period – would not allow Israel to fall prey to the Arabs." [10] This assumption, in Rabbi Amital's view, was proven false: "As to the aid that might have been expected from the 'cultured Christian world,' we may as well not waste words. The picture that was revealed to us is clear, explicit and harsh in all its cruelty." [11]

Rabbi Amital utters his sharpest statements against the nations of the world where he places the entire world on one side – the

cause especially in regard to this aberration of human endeavor, there is no individual without the whole" ("Forty Years Later," p. 85).

8. Genesis Rabbah, *Lekh Lekha* 41, 8 (Theodor-Albeck edition, p. 414).
9. Rabbi Y. Amital, "Obligations of Conscience," p. 29.
10. *HaMa'alot MiMa'amakim*, p. 34.
11. Ibid.

murderers and their assistants, and the nation of Israel on the other side – the victims:

> …in the days when I saw myself amongst the family of the murdered, while on the other side the entire world belonged to the family of the murderers – whether they were active murderers or people who stood silently by while children were killed.[12]

This is one of the most important lessons of the Holocaust:

> Are you really speaking of a lesson? You want to ensure Jewish survival. What took place in the Holocaust – its foundation and basis – was that we stood against the world; all the world on one side, Abraham the Hebrew and us on the other side. This basic situation continues to exist.[13]

In a sermon built on several layers of midrashic interpretations, Rabbi Amital describes Israel's isolation, which is – as it were – an image of the isolation of the Master of the Universe. And He, the Holy One, is the "grandfather," as it were, whose attributes are passed down to His grandchildren:

> Jacob stands facing a hostile world and battles alone against the prince of Esau (Gen. 32:25), who represents all the physical, brutal power in the world. If he had any friends, they were on the other side of the river. Jacob is forced to fight alone, and our Sages see a parallel and similarity here to the "Grandfather," the Holy One; just as He is alone there, so he (Jacob) is alone here…[14]

12. "A World Built," p. 12; also in similar wording in "A Kaddish," p. 8.
13. "A World Built," p. 17.
14. "Just as it is written concerning the Holy One, 'He shall be elevated alone

At the time when Jacob remained alone, it was specifically then that the strength of His God is revealed – it
is then that "God shall be elevated (*nisgav*) alone on
that day" (Isaiah 2:121) is revealed. It is then that it is
revealed to Jacob himself that his strength is not of the
same sort as that of Esau. It is not measured by the
number of weapons that he possesses; his advantage lies
in "the God of Jacob, Selah"… "It is a nation that shall
dwell alone, it shall not be counted among the nations"
(Numbers 23:9)![15]

These words were uttered immediately after the Yom Kippur
War. Where does the story of Jacob end, and the war begin? Where
does the latter end and the Holocaust begin? Where does the verse
end and its exposition begin? And where does the exposition of the
Sages end, and that of Rabbi Amital begin? All are intertwined. Let
us pay attention to a few lines that follow after the above excerpt:

Indeed, in this situation of Jacob fighting alone, there
is an exaltedness that contains something of the Divine
exaltedness. It is not a loftiness of this world. The inner power that is revealed in Jacob at the time when he
remains alone is a sort of Divine strength. The power
of God alone being exalted.[16]

A view of the upper world as reflecting the lower world (and
vice versa) fits in well with other statements by Rabbi Amital, not
only concerning the solitariness and loneliness of God and of the
nation of Israel, but also concerning the content of this unique status. Rabbi Amital claims that the universal destiny of the nation
of Israel is a life of moral behavior that assumes that "Beloved is

(*levado*)' (Isaiah 2:11), so Jacob 'remains alone (*levado*)' (Genesis 32:24)"
(Genesis Rabbah, *Vayishlah* 77, 1 [Theodor-Albeck edition, p. 910]).
15. *HaMa'alot MiMa'amakim*, pp. 50–51.
16. Ibid., p. 50.

man" – every man – "for he was created in God's image,"[17] and that man is required to cleave to God's attributes of mercy.[18]

b. "The Way of Israel"

The term "Jewish morality" is used by Jews to express the entire spectrum of moral views and commandments that, to their minds, are to be found in the Jewish religion and in Jewish tradition.[19] This term, as employed by both religious and secular Jews, is a function of Jewish self-image. The self-image of "merciful people who perform kindnesses" is what defines their moral obligation. Thus we find that Maimonides, for example, goes so far as to cast aspersions on the genealogy of one who does not behave in this manner, and there can be no clearer definition of identity than this:

> Anyone who has within him brazenness or cruelty, who hates others and does not perform kindness towards them, is greatly suspect of being a Gibeonite, for the signs of Israel, the holy nation, are that they are bashful, merciful and perform kindnesses.[20]
>
> It is prohibited for a person to be cruel and not to be appeased; rather, he should be easy to appease and slow to anger… this is the way of the seed of Israel and their sound heart.[21]

17. Mishnah, *Avot* 3:14.
18. See Rabbi Y. Amital, "Minorities."
19. Tradition includes and is subject to many different interpretations, and therefore this term is bound to give rise to sharp disagreement as to its content. See Luz, pp. 214–220. We are concerned here with a description of the moral views and commandments, and with ways of dealing with actual moral problems, rather than with philosophical ethics. See: Luz, p. 216. Some of the concepts that we shall employ in this chapter were coined and defined by him.
20. Maimonides, Laws of Prohibited Sexual Relations, 19:17. See ibid., 12:24, and similarly Laws of Gifts to the Poor, 10:2, where Maimonides applies this definition to "all of Israel and those who join themselves to them." See also Rabbi Jacob ben Asher, *Arba Turim, Even ha-Ezer*, 2.
21. Maimonides, Laws of Repentance, 2:10. See also Maimonides's statement

This image creates an obligation to act in accordance with the "measure of piety" (*middat hasidut*) – even if the law does not explicitly require such behavior. Ehud Luz[22] notes the fact that, according to Maimonides, the full significance of the self-image contained in the expression "Israel's way" creates a moral obligation in a place where no halakhic obligation exists.[23]

Rabbi Amital claims that moral obligation is part of the national identity of the Jewish People, the identity of a nation whose kings are merciful kings[24] and perform many kindnesses. These principles arise in Rabbi Amital's teachings over the course of many years and, as we have seen, they are accentuated and strengthened against the background of the Holocaust.[25]

Rabbi Amital addresses the view that natural moral obligations are the cornerstone of national Jewish identity in an article on Rabbi Kook's statements about this issue.[26] This article is not a theoretical analysis of Rabbi Kook's teachings, but rather an attempt to clarify points that have modern and vital relevance.[27] Rabbi Amital selects a portion of Rabbi Kook's teachings "that seems to deal with

in Laws of Slaves, 9:8: "Cruelty and brazenness exist only in idolaters, but the seed of Abraham our father – and they are Israel, whom the Holy One, Blessed be He, has endowed with the favor of the Torah and commanded with righteous statutes and laws – they are merciful towards everyone."

22. Luz, p. 217.

23. Despite the tendency to include that which is "beyond the letter of the law" within the law itself. See: Rabbi A. Lichtenstein, "Does Judaism Recognize an Ethic Independent of Halakhah?" in his *Leaves of Faith, volume 2: The World of Jewish Living* (Jersey City, 2004); Luz, p. 217–8.

24. 1 Kings 20:31.

25. Rabbi Amital relates to moral behavior as characterizing and identifying the unique image of the nation of Israel even in the course of regular speech, in a sermon on an entirely different topic. See: Rabbi Y. Amital, "How Shall I Ascend to My Father, When the Boy is Not With Me..." (discourse for Shabbat parashat Vayigash 5759), *Alon Shevut Bogrim* 13, 1999, pp. 9–13. In this sermon, over the course of two pages Rabbi Amital mentions such concepts as "moral image," "the unique image of the nation of Israel" and so forth, interchangeably.

26. "Ethical Foundations."

27. Ibid., pp. 16.

a general problem which bears no connection to the realities of his day. Yet, after careful study, it becomes clear that it is anchored in his nationalist and Zionist perception, and it has great significance precisely in our time."[28] This statement indicates the importance of this subject for understanding Rabbi Amital's own ideology. In the article, Rabbi Amital highlights Rabbi Kook's view concerning moral obligations that are not codified in normative Jewish law:

> Moral duties that we are accustomed to define merely as pious deeds, or beyond the letter of the Law, are thus found to be the essence of the Torah.[29]

Rabbi Amital explains that, to Rabbi Kook's view, these obligations have a certain advantage over obligatory laws:

> ... [I]t is desirable that these supererogatory deeds be performed out of an autonomous inner compulsion as a form of free-will offering and an expression of the love of kindness... [T]he ideal is to keep the Torah as the Patriarchs kept it, that is, out of a free, inner cognition, and not by strength of a heavenly command.[30]

This is not just a matter of individual awareness and conscience, but also a guiding principle in Jewish national destiny:

> This great destiny ... is what gives meaning and significance to Jewish existence; it is planted in the depths of the Jew's inner consciousness; it is the source of his longing for redemption.[31]

In other words, it is specifically the moral obligations that are

28. Ibid.
29. Ibid., p. 23 (see Maimonides, Laws of Repentance, 2:10).
30. Ibid.
31. Ibid., p. 18.

defined as "the measure of piety" and as lying "beyond the letter of the Law" that define the Jewish national identity. This is both an inner self-definition and an outward destiny:

> In other words, if all the moral duties were to be turned into mandatory Halakhah, it would be detrimental to Israel's mission of being a light to the nations. It is the very fact that the people of Israel reached, through the Torah's guidance, a moral way of life out of a free inner awareness, that will cause many nations to marvel and will inspire them to ascend to the mountain of the Lord. This is "the Torah [that] will go forth from Zion" and this is the "word of the Lord [which will emanate] from Jerusalem."[32]

Paradoxically, it is specifically the fact that the command to "love your neighbor as yourself," for example, is directed – according to its halakhic definition – only towards Jews, and specifically the fact that "the superficiality of several laws"[33] and of a few statements of the Sages appear to direct one's love of others to Jews only, that make the national morality directed towards other peoples into a mitzvah that arises from the ideal place from which a moral act should arise – the free, inner awareness, and not heteronomous Divine command. It is not defined by the boundaries of Halakhah because "The love of fellow men must burst forth from the source of lovingkindness."[34]

Rabbi Amital emphasizes these components of Rabbi Kook's philosophy. The principle of universal, natural morality – morality that is directed by the Jewish people towards everyone, and which is required of everyone – stands at the foundation of Jewish nationalism. This is not a nationalism that limits goodness and kindness

---

32. Ibid., p. 23.
33. RAYH Kook, *Lights of Holiness*, III, Jerusalem 1974, p. 318 [Hebrew].
34. Ibid.

to itself, but rather one that brings goodness to all. It is unable to bear "any hatred or injustice, nor any limitation or shrinking of goodness and lovingkindness."[35] This natural morality is the crux of the Torah. And "when the people of Israel will succeed in bringing this message to the world, mankind will be healed."[36] These moral foundations are a cornerstone in Rabbi Kook's national and Zionist perception, and they are the reason for and destiny of Jewish national existence.

It should be emphasized that Rabbi Amital quotes one of Rabbi Kook's teachings which, at the time, was not accorded the proper weight and attention: "it is precisely in our days that we can understand them in all their depth and recognize their actual and vital significance."[37] Although Rabbi Amital does not provide an explicit reference in his statement as to the practical relevance and vitality of Rabbi Kook's words, he hints again and again at its significance throughout the article.[38] At the beginning of the article, Rabbi Amital points to a number of events that have exerted a great influence on our times, events which Rabbi Kook never foresaw. These include the Holocaust and the Israeli-Arab wars. From here Rabbi Amital goes on to examine how these two phenomena would have influenced Rabbi Kook's teachings. The parts of his teachings that have become especially relevant are the moral principles contained

---

35. Ibid., p. 349; Rabbi Amital, ibid., p. 18.
36. Rabbi Amital, ibid.
37. Ibid., p. 16.
38. Elsewhere, in a panel discussion organized ten years later with the same title as this article, Rabbi Amital explains the point of contact between Rabbi Kook's words and our reality in terms of modern relevance: "Do you know what the most common word is in Rabbi Kook's writings? Not 'the Land of Israel,' you can check; it is the word 'morality,' which appears almost everywhere. And who speaks today about Rabbi Kook's morality? Nothing so important has yet been written concerning one's attitude towards non-Jews as we find in Rabbi Kook's writings. At the same time, Kahanists speak in the name of Rabbi Kook. Did you see the 'Death to the Arabs' graffiti sprayed all along the road to here? They all speak as though they are disciples of Rabbi Kook" (*Alon Shevut Bogrim* 8, 1996, p. 137). Another discussion of this topic is to be found in "Religious Significance."

within his nationalist ideal, promising a nationalism that will not lead to moral degeneration and a belief in the use of force, belligerence and violence.

The practical application of these ideas receives expression in a letter and a discourse originating in September 1983, relating to current events during the period of the Lebanon War:[39]

> The fact that these thoughts[40] are inserted into verses, statements of the Sages and expressions borrowed from the style of Rabbi Kook, of blessed memory, ... makes me shudder.[41]
>
> Amongst the public one gets the impression... that this world-view is based on the teachings of Rabbi Kook, of sainted memory. My heart is pained over the desecration of Rabbi Kook's honor; how great is the distance between the light that shines forth from his teachings and the spirit that emanates from the above-mentioned utterances and publications. Anyone who is convinced, as I am, that an injustice is being done to the teachings of our masters and teachers who have illuminated the world – Rabbi A.Y. ha-Kohen Kook and Rabbi Y.M. Harlap, of sainted memory – may he be silent? And if he may, *can* he be silent? The Name of

39. "Political" and "Letter." The Lebanon War broke out at the beginning of the summer of 1982. The discourse "A Political or an Educational Message" was delivered on October 6, 1982, and the letter was sent in September of the same year. They explicitly address the war and its events, the slaughter by the Phalangists in Sabra and Shatilla, the public debate concerning the entry into Beirut, and the reactions amongst the Israeli public, especially the Religious Zionist public.

40. The reference here is to political stances that assumed a religious ideological basis ("We went to war in order to enforce order... the world order will be determined by us;" the obligation to enter Beirut without hesitation; support for the bombing of Beirut with no moral deliberation).

41. "Political," p. 39.

Heaven is desecrated, for our many sins; is it possible to be silent!?[42]

In a similar context, Rabbi Amital writes in a letter: "It pains me that such words emanate from a learned Torah scholar and are attributed, directly or indirectly, to Rabbi Kook, of blessed memory, and to Rabbi Harlap, of blessed memory."[43] Rabbi Amital points to sources where Rabbi Kook speaks about man's natural morality, upon which his fear of heaven should be based, and about the value of love of all of humanity.[44]

The emphasis on the moral dimension of Jewish identity and of the moral demands placed on the Jewish nation have assumed an increasingly central place in Rabbi Amital's thought. In fact, Rabbi Amital has gone so far as to reject the identification of the real State of Israel with Rabbi Kook's ideal state that is "the foundation of God's throne in this world,"[45] since the State of Israel fails to meet our moral expectations (as well as for other reasons). In other words, the centrality of Jewish morality does not sit well with the Religious Zionist ideology that relates to the State of Israel as "the foundation of God's throne in the world." The political and ideological significance of such a statement is clear. Rabbi Amital's stance in this regard is consistent, and has become increasingly strong in recent years.

c. Confronting other Religious Zionist Views

These ideas, repeated over and over by Rabbi Amital, should be compared with statements by other Religious Zionist leaders who draw their inspiration from the teachings of Rabbi A.Y. Kook.[46]

42. Ibid., p. 41.
43. "Letter" p. 61.
44. RAYH Kook, *Lights of Holiness*, III, Introduction, #11, p. 27 [Hebrew]; ibid., p. 318; also *The Teachings of Your Father*, Jerusalem 1971, p. 94 [Hebrew].
45. "The State of Israel, the foundation of God's throne in this world, whose entire aim is that God should be One and His name one" (RAYH Kook, *Orot Yisrael*, p. 160).
46. Rabbi Shlomo Aviner declares, at the end of an article that I shall address below, that everything that he says is drawn from the teachings of Rabbi Kook:

Rabbi Shlomo Aviner, for example, wrote the following in an article in the winter of 1975,[47] which was published again in the following years:[48]

> Just as the commandment to conquer the land takes precedence over the principle of "You shall live by them" [i.e., the safeguarding of life], so it takes precedence over the human-moral considerations of the national rights of non-Jews to our land... For all the morality and all the justice whose source is in the hearts of the righteous people of the world has no existence whatsoever except through its being nourished by the word of God. This principle was proclaimed before all the nations in the binding of Isaac, which clarified absolutely the supremacy of Divine command over morality. If man is indeed commanded to perform righteousness and justice, it is only because the Creator of the universe so specified. Our morality is not a human creation, it is not an autonomous morality, but rather imposed from without – to put it more accurately, it is a theonomous morality.[49]

"I declare that everything that is written here contains not a single word of my own; I drew all of it from the fountain of Rabbi Kook, of blessed memory, and especially from my Rabbi and teacher, Rabbi Zvi Yehudah, and his disciples – my teachers" (Aviner, "Realism," p. 65).

47. The journal *Morashah* opened its doors to internal debate within the Religious Zionist camp. Y.Y. Yovel criticizes the tendency towards "Religious Zionist Messianism" ("Religious Zionist Messianism," *Morashah* 9, 1975, pp. 49–54 [Hebrew]), and Rabbi Aviner's statement quoted above is a response to his stance: "The political-theological perception that regards our activities as a decisive stage in the process of redemption relieves itself of the need to address the moral problems that arise from these activities... He sees here only the great historical justice of the redemption of Israel, without the ability to recognize the small injustices that may arise from it" (Y.Y. Yovel, ibid., p. 51).

48. *Artzi* 4, 1983, pp. 30–32 [Hebrew]; Aviner, *Lavi*, vol. 2, pp. 190–196.

49. Aviner, "Realism," p. 65. A. Sagi relates this stance to a political context: "Hence it is reasonable to assume that it is the political context that gives rise

Rabbi Avraham Shapira, who served as Chief Rabbi of Israel from 1983 to 1993, likewise identifies morality absolutely with Halakhah:

> Morality is really Halakhah. We must get used to the fact that Halakhah is natural, it is the reality and the way of life that is required of us... the sole and necessary way of life... It is what determines what is morality.[50]

Elsewhere Rabbi Amital returns to this issue, in direct polemic with views prevalent in the Religious Zionist camp. Rabbi Amital places what the Religious Zionist community views as "Halakhah" and as "commandments" in juxtaposition with the need to guard oneself from moral degeneration. The fact that what is involved is a commandment – or appears to be a commandment – does nothing to prevent damage to one's character:

> Rabbi Shlomo Aviner rejects the claim that the occupation [of the areas captured in the Six-Day War] corrupts us, for conquest of the land is a commandment and it is impossible that fulfillment of a commandment is corruptive. Maimonides, in contrast, writes that King David was tainted with cruelty because of the many wars that he fought, although they fell into the category of obligatory warfare.[51]

---

to the position under discussion" (A. Sagi, *Judaism: Between Religion and Morality*, Tel Aviv 1998, p. 73 [Hebrew]).

50. Rabbi A. Shapira, "War and Morality" (interview), in *Tehumin* 4, 1983, p. 181 [Hebrew]. A. Sagi (*Judaism: Between Religion and Morality*) describes the position described here as one that "tends to reject standard moral considerations in favor of the general principle according to which God, and only God, is the legislator of moral law" (p. 73). Sagi and others contrast this position with others; see A. Sagi (ibid.), especially chapters 1–4, 13–14; Statman *&* Sagi, "Dependence;" *Religion*, pp. 157–164; Luz, pp. 232–4, and the literature that he reviews there and pp. 216–7 and notes.

51. "Not Everything," p. 98.

Rabbi Amital argues with those who place at the center of Religious Zionist education Nahmanides' statement that the commandment of conquering the land and settling it applies to all generations,[52] while they ignore the ramifications of showing preference for one halakhic opinion without addressing other considerations:

> Zionism itself has been defined in terms of halakhic obligation… Nahmanides' statement concerning the settlement of the land has been interpreted by certain circles, as we know, as entailing the adoption of a political position that absolutely prohibits territorial compromise with regard to the Land of Israel… for if Halakhah has had its say, there is no room for any other consideration… [They believe] it is impossible for Halakhah to have negative ramifications, for it is Divine truth.[53]

In this area, as in others, Rabbi Amital warns against turning the deep, inner content of our relationship with the land into a technical, halakhic issue:

> Destruction comes when we turn the Torah into "law" and lose its ethical aspect, that which is "beyond the letter of the law." The Land of Israel, too, can be turned into an halakhic issue, but at the same time one loses the relationship with the Land of Israel as a "homeland."[54]

According to Rabbi Amital, Religious Zionism deals with the question of openness to Enlightenment values and secular culture, and involvement in all areas of modernity, through an exaggerated dependence on Halakhah. Under these conditions, Halakhah serves

52. Nahmanides' additions to *The Book of Commandments*, positive commandment #4.
53. "Not Everything," pp. 97–98.
54. "Guardian of Israel," p. 51.

as "a stable anchor whose function is to guard the purity of Judaism even within the modern world."[55] Rabbi Amital proposes an additional anchor: moral identity.

These themes – the warning against moral degeneration and the opposition to an ideology of using force – bring us back to subjects that were at the center of public debate during the very earliest years of the Zionist movement. The claim that the content and destiny of Jewish nationalism were the moral vision that it bears was raised during the Zionist movement's infancy.[56] This question has retained its relevance, and was imbued with fresh meaning during the course of the century. Rabbi Amital quotes Rabbi Kook as follows:

> Nationalist feeling ... when it is not properly directed and does not turn to the higher goal ... will eventually burst the bounds of morality when it oversteps its boundaries by raising a hand to capture castles that do not belong to it, without righteous judgment and with no holy goal or purpose.[57]

55. "Not Everything," p. 96.
56. Such, for example, was the view of Ahad ha-Am, and he argued for this. See: Ahad ha-Am, "The National Morality," *Collected Writings of Ahad ha-Am*, Tel Aviv 1975, p. 159 ff. [Hebrew]; see also A. Shapira (*Land and Power: The Zionist Resort to Force, 1881–1948*, New York, 1992) and also "The Image of the New Jew in the Early Zionist Society," in *Major Changes Within the Jewish People in the Wake of the Holocaust*, Jerusalem: Yad Vashem, 1993, p. 427–41; E. Schweid, *Judaism and Secular Culture*, Tel Aviv 1981, chapters 1–2 and *Towards a Modern Jewish Culture*, Tel Aviv 1995, chapters 17–18 [Hebrew]; Luz. Ahad ha-Am's basic assumptions were very different from those of Rabbi Kook. Concerning the distance between them, see B. Kurtzweil, *Our New Literature – Continuation or Revolution?* Tel Aviv 1971, p. 190 onwards [Hebrew]. Kurtzweil maintains that Ahad ha-Am's view concerning "a Godless theology... the belief in a Chosen Nation without a Chooser... the prophecy of an emissary without a Sender," and the ranking of the desire for existence and the modern national idea as a supreme value, are what bear the fruits of violence and aggression (ibid., p. 219).
57. RAYH Kook, *Olat Reiyah*, I, Jerusalem 1985, p. 234 [Hebrew].

Rabbi Amital repeats and emphasizes this idea, with reference to the contemporary situation:

> It is worth emphasizing that these things are said with reference to nationalism in Israel; that is, Jewish nationalism which is divorced from the vision of universal redemption is likely to wither to the point of breaking the bounds of morality and seizing castles that do not belong to it, with no justice or righteousness.[58]

3. SANCTIFICATION OF GOD'S NAME AND DESECRATION OF GOD'S NAME

The obligation of moral behavior is included within the obligation to sanctify God's Name (*kiddush ha-Shem*), and within the obligation to avoid desecration God's Name (*hillul ha-Shem*):

> Israel's actions towards the nations of the world are measured in categories of *kiddush ha-Shem* and *hillul ha-Shem*, and therefore any immoral behavior by a Jew towards a non-Jew is a more serious offense than it would be if directed towards another Jew.[59]

Rabbi Amital repeats the combination of concepts "*kiddush ha-Shem*" and "*hillul ha-Shem*" frequently: regarding the "*hillul ha-Shem*" of the Holocaust; regarding his demand of Jews, the State of Israel and especially students and adherents of Torah to behave in such a way as to be a "*kiddush ha-Shem*" as individuals amongst the nation of Israel, and as a nation among the other nations. Behavior that is moral and worthy of admiration on the part of those who study and observe the Torah is a *kiddush ha-Shem*, for they are

58. "Ethical Foundation," p. 20.
59. "Minorities," p. 343. Rabbi Amital discusses this issue with additional halakhic sources in his "Letter," pp. 58–62. For another example of the centrality of this principle in Rabbi Amital's thinking, see adjacent to note 66 below.

called by God's Name. The fate of the nation of Israel, which is
called by God's Name, may likewise cause a *kiddush ha-Shem* or a
hillul ha-Shem.

The concepts *"kiddush ha-Shem"* and *"hillul ha-Shem"* designate the way in which God's Name is viewed in public. These
concepts relate to image as well as the creators of the image; they
describe not necessarily the reality, but rather the way in which
the reality is perceived by the public.[60] The demand for *kiddush
ha-Shem* is also directed towards God, as it were.[61] Rabbi Amital
speaks about how the Holocaust itself was a *hillul ha-Shem*, just as
the establishment of the State was a sanctification of the Name of
Heaven.[62] Behavior that obeys internal, natural morality is behavior that sanctifies the name of Heaven, and it appears that in Rabbi
Amital's view, obedience to natural morality and *kiddush ha-Shem*
are two sides of the same coin.[63]

The obligation of *kiddush ha-Shem* and the prohibition of
hillul ha-Shem apply to every individual in the eyes of the community, to the community in the eyes of other groups,[64] and to the

60. This idea arises from the examples brought by the Talmudic sages to illus-
trate the concept (*Yoma* 86a), as discussed by Rabbi Amital in his "Letter,"
p. 61: "It is explained there that what matters is not the reality but rather the
image; this is simple to understand." The same idea arises from what Rabbi
Amital told an American rabbi, as quoted in the course of a panel discussion:
"It doesn't matter whether it's just or not; the fact is that it involves *hillul ha-
Shem*" (*Alon Shevut Bogrim* 9, 1996, p. 175).
61. See above, Chapter Two, note 176.
62. The concepts of *"hillul ha-Shem"* and *"kiddush ha-Shem"* were broadened
during the course of the generations, assuming additional meanings. See
Maimonides, Laws of the Foundations of Torah 5:10; s.v. *"Hillul ha-Shem"*
in the *Talmudic Encyclopedia*, vol. 15, cols. 340–360 [Hebrew]. The obligation
of *kiddush ha-Shem* stretches to the obligation to give up one's life, under
certain circumstances: Maimonides, *Book of Commandments*, positive commandment #9, negative commandment #63. Concerning *kiddush ha-Shem*
by sacrificing one's life see Urbach, p. 356 ff, as well as an important collection of articles: Y. Gafni and A. Ravitzky (eds.), *Sanctification of Life and
Self-Sacrifice*, Jerusalem 1993 [Hebrew].
63. "Political," pp. 41–42.
64. "Letter," p. 60–61.

nation of Israel and the State of Israel in the eyes of the nations of the world:

> ... Israel's army represents the nation of Israel. The State of Israel has no other function but to sanctify the Name of Heaven... that this nation has the mission of bringing the entire world under the yoke of the Kingdom of Heaven... Anyone who does not recognize this – that the State of Israel, although still in the earliest stages of redemption, is leading towards having many nations coming and saying, "Let us go and walk in the light of God" (Isaiah 2:5), someone who severs this obligation from the State of Israel – has no portion in Religious Zionism. The purpose of the Jewish State is not to solve the problem of Jewish existence... the Guardian of Israel is the One who will protect the remainder of Israel. If we have a mission, it is the sanctification of the Name of Heaven. And the Holy One says to us: If we have any language with which to speak to the Shiites and the Gibeonites, it is the language of kindness, of performing justice, that they may say – "The kings of Israel are merciful kings."[65]

In a lecture on the Torah's attitude towards minorities, Rabbi Amital claims that since the State of Israel's Declaration of Independence promises equal rights to minorities, failing to fulfill this promise is a *hillul ha-Shem*, and therefore the existence of the Declaration of Independence has a "halakhic weight over

---

65. "Obligations of Conscience," p. 30. These words were uttered on June 23, 1985 (see ibid., p. 23). It seems that Rabbi Amital's perception of the subject of *hillul ha-Shem* influences his fear of the moral degeneration that occupation may cause. See his dispute with Rabbi Aviner, above. It is from here that Rabbi Amital's protest arose, during the period of the Lebanon War, against militant and aggressive views, as discussed above.

and above many other laws."[66] In other words, the Declaration of Independence assumes halakhic weight, which should be granted priority because of the considerations of *kiddush ha-Shem* and *hillul ha-Shem*.[67]

It appears that this was the source of Rabbi Amital's outcry following the Sabra and Shatilla massacres. The question of the factual reality is irrelevant when there is clearly an instance of *hillul ha-Shem*. *Hillul ha-Shem* is whatever looks like a *hillul ha-Shem*, regardless of the facts. What took place looked like it happened under the responsibility of the State of Israel, and it contradicted

66. "Minorities," p. 341. For further discussion and halakhic sources on this issue, see "Letter" pp. 58–62.

67. The discourse did not deal with Halakhah in the formal sense, but rather proposed values that should guide "our attitude, behavior and actions" (ibid., p. 343), values that have binding halakhic weight (*kiddush ha-Shem* and the avoidance of *hillul ha-Shem*; the universal destiny of the nation of Israel; "Its ways are ways of pleasantness and all its paths are peace;" "Precious is man, who was created in the Divine Image;" cleaving to the attributes of the Holy One, Who is good to all). A halakhic authority has Halakhah on one side, and the reality and his understanding of it on the other. Beyond the technical tools, there is a comprehensive view of the world, a picture of reality and a vision of the future. Recently Rabbi Amital has addressed these questions with criticism of halakhic rulings based on the formal use of halakhic precedent, with no regard for general principles such as "You shall be holy," "You shall perform that which is upright and that which is good," and criticism also of political use of Halakhah. See, for example: Rabbi Y. Amital, "Political Opinion Enveloped in Halakhah," *Meimad* 5, 1995, pp. 6–7; his speech at the Religious Zionist Conference, October 28, 1996 (= Rabbi Y. Amital, "Soul-Searching," *Alon Shevut Bogrim* 8, 1996, pp. 11–14); and recently "Not Everything is Halakhah"). For a discussion pertinent to this topic, see his article "Da'at Torah." Rabbi Amital argued against other rabbis who issued halakhic rulings in political matters, and noted that there are some who prefer halakhic rulings originating in certain circles to halakhic rulings from other circles, with such preferences invariably matching their political preferences for those rabbis. Rabbi Amital also expresses concern for the fact that Halakhah has become a means to present political views, and draws our attention to the social ramifications of basing a political view upon halakhic claims: we are thereby prevented from engaging in genuine dialogue with the secular population on the most existential questions occupying the nation in Israel.

the essence of Judaism. This Rabbi Amital could not accept, and it seems to have been a most important turning point in his teachings and activities.

Rabbi Amital recounts how he tried to have Rabbi Goren's article on Jewish warfare in light of Halakhah reprinted.[68] A study of the article brings us back to some of the principles discussed above. Rabbi Goren distinguishes between halakhic justice – which believes that "justice shall break the mountain" (i.e., the law must be upheld at all costs) – and moral justice: "And in everything pertaining to taking human life, there is a teaching of the pious ones that sometimes contradicts Halakhah … and in this area we must follow this teaching of the pious ones."[69] This applies even to the lives of non-Jews: "The 'teaching of the pious ones' is based on the trait of mercy, in accordance with which we must act even in war, and which we learn from the traits of the Holy One, Blessed be He."[70] Rabbi Amital continues as follows:

> [Rabbi Goren] insisted that the war be waged on the highest moral level… He proves that according to Halakhah the civilian population should not be harmed – certainly, one is forbidden to harm women or children. Even the enemy may not be harmed beyond the degree required for victory or for self-defense… These words are important specifically in our times, when we hear from his students – who did not learn from him all that they needed to – statements such as, "The blood of non-Jews is ownerless"… I be-

---

68. Rabbi Y. Amital, "Woe to the Land of Israel, Lacking Great Men" (*Alon Shevut Bogrim* 6, 1995, p. 126). Rabbi Amital refers here to an article by Rabbi S. Goren, "The Morality of War in Light of Halakhah," *Meshiv Milhamah*, vol. 1, Jerusalem 1983, pp. 3–40 [Hebrew].
69. Rabbi S. Goren, ibid., p. 28.
70. Ibid.

lieve it is imperative that this be published specifically in our times.[71]

* * *

There can be no doubt that this moral sensitivity is strengthened by the memory of the Holocaust, by the desire not to be a murderer as expressed in his heartfelt blessing during the Holocaust, "…Who has not made me a gentile." The Holocaust gave rise to a demand for moral behavior, and a cry of protest against the *hillul ha-Shem* that comes about through behavior that is otherwise.[72]

The moral essence is what characterizes Jewish identity; this is "the way of Israel." This identifying trait found its boldest expression in the period of the Holocaust. As explained above, in some of Rabbi Amital's statements there is an echo of Rabbi Yehudah's words in Genesis Rabbah: "Abram [was called] the 'Hebrew' (*ivri*) … for all the world was on one side (*ever*), and he was on the other."[73]

> Facing a world of murderers, a world that stood by as the blood of millions was shed – we stood on the other side; all the world on one side and we on the other.[74]

4. ATTITUDE TOWARDS SECULAR JEWS IN THE WAKE OF THE HOLOCAUST

During the course of a discussion on the halakhic and religious status of secular Jews in our times, Rabbi Amital raises considerations related to the Holocaust and its trauma. Rabbi Amital claims that the Holocaust presents a challenge to faith, and that those who have not met the challenge successfully should not be judged.

Here Rabbi Amital bases his approach on that of Rabbi Kook.

---

71. Rabbi Amital, ibid.
72. See, for example: "Political."
73. Genesis Rabbah, *Lekh Lekha*, 41, 8 (Theodor-Albeck edition, p. 414).
74. "A Kaddish," p. 8.

Rabbi Kook maintained that children who have strayed from the path should be regarded as having been "coerced" by the "current of time," or the spirit of the age.[75] Rabbi Amital likewise believes that we must distinguish between those who have adopted heresy out of willfulness and those who are to be considered as having been "coerced."[76] He adds that if this was the case during the lifetime of Rabbi Kook, prior to the Holocaust, it is certainly true after the Holocaust:

> What shall we say after the Holocaust? Are we permitted to condemn people who find it difficult to have faith after all that the Holocaust did to Jewish souls? If Rabbi Kook and the Hazon Ish spoke of "coerced innocents" before the Holocaust, what shall we say today?[77]

If someone denies his faith after the Holocaust, it is questionable whether we are able to judge him. Someone who "find[s] it difficult to have faith" after the Holocaust is "coerced in his belief."[78] The Holocaust confronts him and forces him into apostasy. Rabbi Amital here raises the possibility of a lenient approach in our generation towards non-believers. The Holocaust is incorporated into the spiritual makeup of the generation, and this must be addressed by halakhic authorities when they examine contemporary reality. This attitude towards non-believers after the Holocaust has halakhic ramifications.[79]

75. RAYH Kook, *Letters*, 1, #138, p. 171 [Hebrew].
76. "Secular Jews," pp. 40–41.
77. Ibid., p. 41.
78. Attention should be paid to the fact that Rabbi Amital here, as elsewhere, re-examines the relevance of Rabbi Kook's statements for the post-Holocaust period. In this instance, the Holocaust actually strengthens Rabbi Kook's view, following the principle of "how much more so…"
79. An example of a similar consideration is to be found in Rabbi Amital's discussion of the commandment of rebuke, which by its nature turns on social questions and considerations (Rabbi Y. Amital, "Rebuking a Fellow Jew: Theory and Practice," in *Jewish Tradition and the Non-Traditional Jew*, ed. Rabbi

One of the factors influencing halakhic decision-making is the decisor's perception of reality. In Rabbi Amital's view, the spiritual impact of the Holocaust must be factored into the decisor's grasp of current reality; he must recognize that our spiritual perception has changed. It is impossible to address questions of faith – and to deal with the status of secular Jews – without taking into account the damage wreaked by the Holocaust on the souls of Israel, whether consciously or unconsciously. The demands made of a non-believer afterwards are not the same as the demands before.

Later on in the same article, following a halakhic analysis, Rabbi Amital raises further considerations concerning the status of secular Jews in our times. These considerations contribute to the outline of Jewish identity. The first of these is that Jewish identity is also determined by our appearance in the eyes of others:

> There was a time when the Jews were hated for being the bearers of the Torah. As soon as a Jew stopped living according to his religion and accepted the religion of his Gentile milieu, the hatred ceased. This is no longer true. Contemporary Jew-hatred is racial, directed against people in whose veins Jewish blood flows, irrespective of whether they live by the Torah or have had themselves baptized. When Jew-hatred is aimed at a person solely because he is a Jew, regardless of his opinions and actions, so should *ahavat Yisra'el* – love of fellow Jews – also be directed at every Jew solely because he is a Jew, regardless of his opinions and actions. Let no one

Jacob J. Schacter, Northvale, NJ 1992, pp. 119–138; also in *Alei Etzion* 2, 1995, pp. 47–64. Similar to this is the question of including Shabbat-desecrators as part of a *minyan* (Rabbi Y. Amital, "Concerning the Inclusion of Those Who Desecrate Shabbat in Public to Form a *Minyan*," *Alon Shevut* 4:3, 1973, pp. 17–19; also "Concerning One Question," *Reuven: In Memory of Reuven Sporen*, Kfar ha-Roeh 1981, pp. 151–153 [Hebrew]), and questions of *hillul ha-Shem* and *kiddush ha-Shem* – in other words, the way in which the name of God, the Torah, its students and adherents are perceived by others, both Jews and non-Jews (see above, and see "Letter," pp. 55–62).

entertain the notion that someone treated as a Jew by the anti-semites is going to be treated by us as an outsider. Even in the Halakhah we find that although we are not required to bewail the death of an apostate, we do mourn over him if he is killed by Gentiles because of his Jewish origins. In Auschwitz the Germans did not check Jews for their opinions or degrees of observance. Are we going to do so as a preliminary to observing the *mitzvot* of "You shall love your fellow as yourself" and "Your brother shall live with you"?[80]

Rabbi Amital proposes, with regard to identifying the "fellow" the Torah tells us to love and the "brother" with whom the Torah tells us to live, that we adopt the definition of brotherhood provided by our enemies. This is not because he accepts this definition on its own merits, but because he cannot "entertain the notion that someone treated as a Jew by the anti-semites is going to be treated by us as an outsider." Jew-haters have redefined the boundaries of Jewish solidarity.

The State of Israel has religious significance because of the principle of "saving lives" and because of the *kiddush ha-Shem* that it embodies. Therefore, we must consider in halakhic decision-making the influence of halakhic decisions on the State's ability to survive:

> The second consideration concerns mainly the State of Israel, with ramifications pertaining to *pikuach nefesh* – the saving of life. If we believe that the State of Israel is a haven for millions of Jews, and that the survival of those Jews hinges on peace for Israel and the Jewish state's capacity to withstand its many enemies; and if we believe that the reestablishment of the Jewish state and its survival constitute *Kiddush ha-Shem* – sanctification and glorification of God's name; if the State of

80. "Secular Jews," pp. 44–45.

Israel is precious to us; if we have not yet been infected by the "*Haredi* heresy," which excludes God from the history of the reestablishment of Jewish statehood and regards it as a purely human act – then we had better realize that the State of Israel is not going to endure if cordial relations do not prevail between all sectors of the nation. Only if Jews relate to each other as brothers, irrespective of ideology, can we maintain this state. Otherwise, we live under a threat of destruction.[81]

We must be precise in pointing out the halakhic significance of the above. It is defined explicitly: the practical ramification lies in our understanding of the parameters of the commandments of "loving your fellow as oneself" and "Your brother shall live with you." When Rabbi Amital raises the considerations of the attitude of anti-Semites and the strength and durability of the State of Israel, at the conclusion of a typical halakhic analysis, he is well aware of the difficulty of finding support for such considerations in ancient halakhic sources:

I do not have to adduce any source texts to support these latter two considerations. Concerning such instances, the Sages have already said, "Why do I need a quotation from Scripture? It stands to reason."[82]

---

81. Ibid., p. 45.
82. Ibid. Concerning the argument and its validity as an halakhic source, see, for example, Menahem Elon, *Jewish Law: History, Sources, Principles*, Philadelphia 1994, pp. 987–1014. Concerning the argument in the context of our topic, see Statman *&* Sagi, "Dependence," p. 133 ff.

Appendix A

"Has There Ever Been Such a Thing, or Has Such a Thing Been Heard?"[1] Rabbi Amital's Use of Historical Models

THE SOCIAL AND IDEOLOGICAL context in which Rabbi Amital operates, as a Religious Zionist, is exposed to modernity consciously, as a matter of choice.[2] He is exposed to the historical narrative that arises from modern historiography, either in the original or otherwise at second- or third-hand. Nevertheless, when seeking historical models and frameworks, he generally ignores the narrative as recounted by modern historiography, choosing to make use of Jewish traditional historical memory rather than the findings of historical research.

When describing Rabbi Akiva's attitude towards Bar Kokhba,[3] for example, or the actions of Rabban Yohanan ben Zakkai when he left Jerusalem for Yavneh, Rabbi Amital completely ignores the

---

1. Deuteronomy 4:32
2. See Schwartz, *Faith*, p. 176 ff. I described above the Religious Zionist trend of adopting modern historiography for theological purposes.
3. In discussing this attitude, Rabbi Amital uses the description of Maimonides in his Laws of Kings 1:3. Maimonides in turn bases himself on the Jerusalem Talmud and the Midrash. Rabbi Abraham ben David (Rabad) of Posquieres comments on this, and directs us to the corresponding narrative in the Babylonian Talmud. See Maimonides, Laws of Fast Days 5:3. A discussion

findings of historical research in recent generations, although these have long been part of Israeli culture.

The historical narrative and the historical memory within which Rabbi Amital operates are those of Maimonides. He uses Maimonides' historical descriptions as a model according to which he constructs his own historical-theological description. Y.H. Yerushalmi compares collective memory with modern historiography and bemoans the loss of Jewish group memory.[4] In Rabbi Amital we have an example of a living memory molding a religious and traditional world-view that informs his discourses, his vision, his public activities and his religious leadership.[5]

In those instances where Rabbi Amital has attempted to find the religious significance of historical events, he makes use of the historical model found in Jewish tradition as a framework into which he fits the events and from within which he gives them meaning. This approach includes both historical models borrowed from the Bible[6] and models described in Jewish tradition, such as, for example, the historical descriptions of Maimonides. The historical picture drawn by modern historians and scholars is of no interest to him. His historiographic paradigm is that of traditional Jewish

---

of Maimonides' historical description, his formulation and the comments on it, is presented by J. Efron, "The Battle of Bar Kokhba in Light of the Talmudic Tradition – Jerusalem vs. Babylonian," in A. Oppenheimer and A. Rapaport (eds.), *The Bar Kokhba Rebellion – New Studies*, Jerusalem 1984, pp. 47–105 [Hebrew]. For attempts at historical reconstructions of the positions of Rabbi Akiva and the Sages during the Rebellion, see, for example: Gedalyahu Alon, *The Jews in their Land in the Talmudic Age (70–640 CE)*, Jerusalem 1980, p. 630 ff; Urbach, p. 673 ff.; A. Mor, *The Strength and Scope of the Bar Kokhba Rebellion*, Jerusalem 1992, p. 220 ff [Hebrew].

4. Yerushalmi, *Zakhor*.
5. The traditional historical memory is often liable to be nourished by the findings of historical research, but Rabbi Amital declines even this opportunity; he is content with the narrative presented by Maimonides.
6. "We cannot fit the establishment of the State of Israel into any verse of Bible other than those that speak of the Return to Zion" ("Guardian of Israel," p. 52).

memory. Rabbi Amital is interested only in the story as it is told in Jewish tradition, and in the portrait of the world and the moral and religious attitude that this memory involves.

The entire discussion is conducted with a historiographic consciousness that is anchored in Jewish tradition and Jewish memory. This is not a memory that has atrophied and lost its strength, but rather a memory that is full of life, that is constantly molding itself and creating anew, and whose influence is greater than that of the work of a modern historian.

The typological use of stories from the Bible or other narratives is accepted in Jewish tradition, and here again Rabbi Amital follows a traditional mode of thought that is reminiscent of the Talmudic Sages.[7]

This is particularly highlighted at the junction where we find those who pretend to understand the ups and downs of our historical situation, attempting to identify therein the imminent redemption. They seek within historical events the signs testifying to the redemption of Israel; they watch for the breaking of the dawn, seeking He who "stands behind our wall, watching through the windows and peeping through the lattice."

It is at this junction of questioning that Rabbi Amital stands. He uses models drawn from Jewish tradition, not historical research, to search for the answer to the question of the time of redemption. He examines the question anew again and again, never ceasing to seek answers. Thus, for example, Rabbi Amital turns to the narrative of Maimonides in his attempt to see the period in which we live

7.   See – out of a great body of literature – an example that is close to the issue under discussion: Y. Heinemann, "Messiah the Son of Ephraim and the Premature Exodus from Egypt of the Tribe of Ephraim," *Tarbiz* 40, 1971, pp. 450–461 [Hebrew]. See also D. Berger, "Three Typological Themes in Early Jewish Messianism: Messiah, Son of Joseph, Rabbinic Calculation, and the Finger of Armilus," *AJS Review* 10, 1985, pp. 141–164. Berger notes that the use of typological exegesis arises from a strong desire to know the events of the times and their essence – a desire that cannot be satisfied by an examination of the explicit texts of biblical prophecy.

as following the model of "the redemption of the Second Temple."[8] He does the same when trying to raise the possibility of error in identifying the redemption and its signs – a possibility of error that echoes the identification of Bar Kokhba as the messiah by Rabbi Akiva. Here too, Rabbi Amital appeals to the historical narrative as presented by Maimonides.[9]

When Rabbi Amital viewed the State of Israel as "the beginning of the flowering of our redemption," he consciously and explicitly employed not a model based on the historical past, but rather the model of future events proposed by Rabbi Kook.[10] Rabbi Amital's desisting from interpreting our time as one of a deterministic redemption also evolved from his examination of Rabbi Kook's model, by attempting to adapt it to recent events, testing it against the Holocaust and against the historical reality from the time of its formulation by Rabbi Kook until today.

8. "Religious Significance," p. 141.
9. Transcript of discourse delivered on Hannukah 1996. See also Maimonides, Laws of Kings 11:3; Laws of Fast Days 5:3.
10. This model itself continues a long tradition of describing and identifying the Messianic Era; see note 7 above.

Appendix B

Moral Obligations Arising
from Inner Recognition

RABBI AMITAL classifies the moral obligations that are not included within the 613 commandments[1] of binding Halakhah as obligations that precede Halakhah and the commandments. "The moral duties that a man assumes out of an inner awareness and the demand of conscience,"[2] and the commitment to "righteousness and justice" – which are the way of God – precede the commitment to observe God's commandments as set forth in Halakhah:

> The first message which Judaism came to convey was that of commitment to justice and righteousness. It is

---

1.   Inner motivation and conscience is needed for these too ("Ethical Foundation," p. 23).

2.   "Ethical Foundation" p. 16. In Rabbi Kook's words: "natural morality which is rooted in man's honest nature" (RAYH Kook, *Lights of Holiness*, III, Introduction, #11, p. 27 [Hebrew]). Rabbi Amital follows Rabbi Kook's lead in this matter. Concerning the existence and status of natural morality in Jewish tradition, and its relationship with Halakhah, see Statman *&* Sagi, "Dependence." With regard to the relationship of dependence between religion and morality see Statman *&* Sagi, *Religion*; Y. Ahituv, *On the Border of Change* [Hebrew], Jerusalem 1995, pp. 341–342, and notes 3–5. See also A. Sagi, *Judaism:Between Religion and Morality*.

said of Abraham our Patriarch: "For I know him, that he will command his children and his household after him, and they shall keep the way of God, to do justice and righteousness" (Genesis 18:19). It doesn't say, "to observe the Lord's commandments," because the commandments hadn't yet been given.[3]

The key to the Jewish essence and to Jewish identity is to be found, first and foremost, in moral behavior that is beyond the letter of the law. Rabbi Amital has frequently emphasized his opposition to propounding a binding legal code in matters of morality. Moral behavior must derive from one's free internal recognition, not from an external obligation:

> There are commandments which a person must fulfill not because he was so commanded by God, but because that is his will and that reflects his inner consciousness... We must know that Halakhah is only an opening, a gateway through which the Holy One transmits a certain message to us, while a large portion of the laws pertaining to human behavior are intended for a person to fulfill out of inner awareness... In the laws of character traits, no code such as the *Shulhan Arukh* is of any use. If the heart has not been mended, no codified law will help him... The purpose of the Torah is that a person should perform and fulfill the Torah as the patriarchs fulfilled it – out of inner awareness.[4]

3. Rabbi Y. Amital, "Social Challenges," p. 12.
4. "Obligations of Conscience," pp. 28–29. Rabbi Amital quotes the Maharal: "If one performs an obligation as though he is fulfilling a royal decree, this is not what the Holy One desires; he should do it out of his own will... if he is forced to do it, then he is not serving Him. Likewise, if he lent money as though he were fulfilling a royal decree, this is not a mitzvah, for the mitzvah of lending must be done willingly, with a good heart" (Maharal, *Gur Aryeh ha-Shalem*, Jerusalem 1992, Exodus 20:22). In Rabbi Amital's view, this

Elsewhere Rabbi Amital identifies the reliance on Halakhah as they way in which Religious Zionism deals with its openness to secular education and culture and its involvement in all spheres of modernity. Under these conditions, Halakhah serves as a "stable anchor whose purpose is to preserve the purity of Judaism, even within the modern world."[5] In addition to this anchor, Rabbi Amital proposes the anchor of moral identity. To his view, the strong emphasis on Halakhah – to the neglect of morality, to some degree – exacts a spiritual price:

> I believe that this excessive emphasis on Halakhah has entailed a somewhat undesirable price. The impression has been created that there is nothing in Torah other than that which exists in Halakhah, and that in addressing any new problem that arises in modern society, answers should be sought solely in the works of Halakhah. Many of the fundamental values of the Torah that are based on the general commandments of "You shall be holy" and "You shall do what is right and good in God's eyes," and that have no explicit instructional formulation, are not only underrated but have lost some of their validity in the eyes of a public that sees itself as obligated to Halakhah… The use made by Religious Zionist ideology of Halakhah, which has become quite intensive in the wake of our political problems, influences the way in which Halakhah is perceived in the eyes of the younger generation, and this has fateful implications for religious life in general.[6]

An example of the preference for moral behavior arising out of inner consciousness is the "study curriculum" in matters of moral-

excerpt served as a foundation for Rabbi Kook in his letter to Dr. M. Seidel (*Letters*, I, #89, pp. 92–101).
5.   "Not Everything," p. 96.
6.   Ibid., pp. 96–97.

ity proposed by Rabbi Amital to one of his students. In response to the student's question, Rabbi Amital suggested that he learn *Mussar* rather than the laws of slander. The technical study of the exact details of the law, without the idea and the value that it contains, is defective,[7] certainly in the case of interpersonal matters:

> Every mitzvah has two levels: there is the halakhic level, and the ethical level. In commandments between man and God we are instructed, "You shall be holy" (Leviticus 19:2), while in commandments between man and his fellow we are instructed, "You shall perform what is right and good" (Deut. 6:18). Nahmanides, in his famous comment (to Lev. 19:2), teaches that it is possible for a person to be a "scoundrel within the bounds of Torah:" he may fulfill all of the laws, while forgetting their ethical aspect. A person may guard himself from transgressing the laws of stealing, but at the same time lose the ethical aspect of loving his fellow man, justice and righteousness. A person may guard himself from speaking slander, but at the same time feel jealousy towards his neighbor, hate him, and rejoice in his failures.[8]

It is instructive to note the way in which Rabbi Amital applies this principle to the commandment of settling the Land of Israel. Here too, as in other areas, he warns against turning our relationship with the land into a technical, halakhic matter:

> One can make the Land of Israel, too, into a halakhic issue, while at the same time losing one's relationship

---

7. Rabbi Y. Amital, "Guard Your Tongue from Evil," *Alon Shevut Bogrim* 6, 1995, p. 11. Rabbi Amital hereby proposes a different path than that of the Hazon Ish.
8. "Guardian of Israel," p. 51.

with the Land of Israel as a "homeland." We must also regard the land in the same way that the non-Jews relate to their own homelands. What is "Jewish sovereignty"? It is the natural feeling that we have our own government… There is no section about this in the *Shulḥan Arukh*, but it is a basic value in our lives.[9]

A view that gives the moral obligations arising from inner consciousness preference over Halakhah, in any sense, does not cohere with the obligation to obey "the word of God – that is Halakhah" (*Shabbat* 138b), which Rabbi Amital demands of his students. Although Rabbi Amital has not fully addressed the internal consistency of his statements, he does address to some degree the difficulties that they create. He demands of his students a commitment to Torah and to serving God:

> Authority and obligation [are] two foundations without which it is difficult to imagine living in accordance with the Torah.[10]
> The Gemara (*Rosh ha-Shanah* 28a) teaches that, "The [commandments] were not given for our enjoyment." Rashi adds: "… they were given to be a yoke upon their necks."[11]

Rabbi Amital does not propose that Halakhah be shunted

9. Ibid.
10. "Commitment," p. 33.
11. Ibid., p. 38. In this discourse Rabbi Amital criticizes those trends that place the world of Torah and the commandments on a basis of complete voluntarism. This subject was already raised in a discourse on the occasion of the 30th anniversary of the yeshivah, where Rabbi Amital sets down the philosophy of the yeshivah and indicates the educational questions that need to be addressed: "The sense of commitment has gradually been ground away in recent years… [people] want to fulfill the Torah based on 'We will do and we will hear,' rather than 'He held the mountain over them like a cask'" ("Understand the Years," p. 140).

aside or that one take from it what he wants, according to the dictates of his inner consciousness. Rather, he demands full commitment to Halakhah.

Rabbi Amital attempts in several ways to bridge the gap between fulfilling commandments out of inner consciousness and commitment to Halakhah. He presents these two paths as lying one adjacent to the other:

> According to our Sages, the Nation of Israel accepted the Torah at Sinai out of two different motivations. The one was a freely-accepted and enthusiastic declaration of "We shall observe and we shall hear" (Ex. 24:7); the other was the coercive and threatening suspension of the Mt. Sinai like a cask over their heads (*Shabbat* 88a). It would seem that nothing could be more ideal than accepting the Torah out of free will and inner conviction ... At the same time, acceptance of the Torah that is based only on willing assent, without a basis of coercion, is deficient.[12]

In an attempt to bridge the distance between the two positions, Rabbi Amital proposes the use of a new term that is located somewhere between commitment and voluntarism. Instead of "commitment," he suggests using the term "loyalty" or "faithfulness." Loyalty includes commitment within itself, but at the same time it feels closer to one's heart.[13] Rabbi Amital himself is aware that this solution is a matter of semantics, but nevertheless it is proposed out of an awareness of the dynamic created by words.[14] The distance between the two positions is further reduced when Rabbi Amital creates an identity between the essence of human nature and the need for loyalty and commitment:

12. "Commitment," p. 35.
13. Ibid., pp. 39.
14. Ibid., p. 42

The story shows that commitment – "loyalty," in [the Sages'] terms – is part of the essence of human nature, and deviation from it is a deviation from human nature… Commitment is not something external; rather, it flows from human nature… A world that revolts against commitment is in fact revolting against its human nature.[15]

Elsewhere, discussing the requirement that one cleave to and emulate the attributes of God, Rabbi Amital again comes back to the question of the source from which moral behavior arises:

This requirement, to cleave to the attributes of the Holy One, is not meant to weaken the natural feelings of kindliness that exist within a person's heart, but rather – on the contrary – to strengthen them; [as Rabbi Kook says,] "The love of fellow men must burst forth from the source of lovingkindness, not as a matter of law, for then the clearest part of its brightness would be lost, but rather as a mighty inner movement of the soul."[16] But since it is clear that "the love distances itself from its Divine source; its blossom withers" (ibid.), it is especially important that goodness, kindness and mercy be based on the requirement to emulate the attributes of the Holy One, which are the traits of mercy.[17]

The strong emphasis that Rabbi Amital places upon natural

---

15. Ibid. There can be no doubt that Rabbi Amital's various statements on this issue are not altogether consistent. We have already pointed out that he has no organized set of teachings, but rather the body of teachings of an educator. Each of his statements exists within its own context, and each is a reaction to a different reality. Rabbi Amital himself tries in this discourse to find some balance between his different statements.
16. RAYH Kook, *Lights of Holiness*, III, p. 318.
17. "Minorities," p. 342.

morality raises a serious problem regarding the Holocaust. It is difficult to speak of "natural morality" together with the loss of faith in man and his morality. Disillusionment with man, as revealed in the Holocaust, may cause – and has caused in many instances – a loss of faith in man altogether, and in morality that is based on man.[18] Rabbi Amital recounts:

> Once I participated in a televised panel discussion with [the partisan and poet] Abba Kovner, concerning the significance of the Holocaust and the profound dilemmas of life thereafter, for the survivors. I said there, inter alia, that these questions are much more terrible for a person who does not believe in God. If there is no choice but to believe in something, then what is left to believe in for a person without God? Can one believe in mankind, after what the German nation and their helpers from the family of nations did? I had a vision of German trains transporting the army to the front, that were stopped and vacated in order to transport Jews to Auschwitz… To believe in man after all that is impossible.[19]

Consolation is not to be found in a place where there is only faith in man. Only faith in the Holy One, with all its perplexities, can bring consolation:

> But my heart goes out to those Jews who have no faith, who say, "I believe in man," and that is what gives them strength. For we have seen how far man can degenerate; happy are we, how good is our portion, that we believe in the Holy One, Blessed be He, concerning Whom it is written, "My thoughts are not your thoughts" (Isaiah

---

18. A. Sagi, p. 70, raises this possibility in his response to S.Z. Shragai.
19. "Nation Before Land," pp. 11–12. Also: "A World Built," p. 13.

55:8), even with all of our questions. But to say, "I believe in man," and to exist like that?[20]

Rabbi Amital formulates this differently, as is his way, in one of his story-discourses:

> After the Shoah, can you still believe in man? I believe in God, Whom I cannot understand. But man should be fathomable – so what do you believe in now?[21]

20. "A Kaddish," p. 9.
21. "Confronting the Holocaust," p. 51.

Appendix C

Forty Years Later: A Personal Recollection

By Rabbi Yehudah Amital[1]

WHEN I WAS FIRST APPROACHED with the idea of holding a festive meal for the entire yeshivah to mark the fortieth anniversary of my *aliyah*, I was a bit hesitant to grant permission. The nature of my *aliyah*, coming as it did towards the end of the Holocaust, has made many of my memories of my *aliyah* extremely painful. However, after carefully considering the repeated requests to honor this occasion, I felt there were two reasons that justified this reception and I therefore gave my consent.

First, and most importantly, I felt that it was an opportunity to thank and praise God, for all the kindness and grace that He has bestowed upon me.

Second, I would like to share with you some of my personal experiences, as these experiences can only add to and heighten our Jewish consciousness. Within the yeshivah, where I find myself among family, close friends, comrades and students, I am willing

---

1. On the fortieth anniversary of Rabbi Amital's *aliyah* to the Land of Israel, a reception was held in Yeshivat Har Etzion, where he spoke with the yeshivah students about the Holocaust and how it affected him. The reception took place on the eve of Rosh Chodesh Adar 5745 (February 21, 1985). This discourse was adapted from a cassette by Aviad Hacohen.

to try to communicate, as best I can, some of these experiences, so that all may benefit from them.

Tonight marks the beginning of the month of Adar. According to the Mishnah (*Shekalim* 1:1), "On the first of Adar, they make proclamation regarding the *shekalim* (the annual donation to the Temple)." The Talmud (*Yerushalmi Shekalim* 1:1) explains this law as follows:

> Why is this done on the first of Adar? In order to allow Israel enough time to bring their *shekalim*, and thus the tithes of the office [which provide for the congregational sacrifices beginning a month later on the first of Nissan] will be supplied from the new [funds] on time.

The Talmud teaches us that we are obligated to pay for the congregational sacrifices from the new tithes that are donated to the Temple. The year begins on the first of Nissan, and in order to ensure that everything is prepared on time, the collection of the half-shekel is begun a month beforehand, on the first of Adar. The congregational sacrifices of the coming year are then purchased with the money raised through the donation of the half-shekel.

In telling us that we may not worship God with the use of the previous year's donations, this law reveals a profound message. Each new year, each new generation, each new era, is marked by its own donations and its own sacrifices. The worship of God from the lofty spiritual height of the Temple is one that contains deep emotional meaning. Any change or deviation, no matter how little, is considered significant. The individual can only present a sacrifice which has been purchased from the new funds. That which belonged to the previous year is no longer valid. It has come to the end of its usefulness.

When the Temple was destroyed, we lost this delicate balance inherent within the nature of our worship of God. We no longer sense the difference, we are no longer cognizant of the inherent change, between one year and the next. Rather we live from generation to generation, from era to era. Upon the verses, "Yet the Lord has not given you a heart to perceive, and eyes to see, and ears to hear, until this day. And I have led you forty years in the wilderness…" (Deut. 29:3–4), the Talmud comments: "From this [verse] we learn that it can take an individual forty years to know the mind of one's master" (*Avodah Zarah* 5b). The entire congregation of Israel was unable to understand the mind of its Master in Heaven until forty years had passed! How much more so is it difficult to understand the mind of our Master during an era that all human logic has failed to comprehend. Yet, it has become clear after such a period of ultimate horror, that this was not a process that concerned only our nation. It was a universal process, an all-embracing dilemma. We must not consider only the individual, because especially in regard to this aberration of human endeavor, there is no individual without the whole.

When my family and I commemorate the day upon which I came to Israel, I am accustomed to combining my thanksgiving for being saved with thanksgiving for my *aliyah*. Indeed, in my mind, both are intrinsically connected. I did not see myself as gaining total salvation when I had escaped from the Nazis. I only came to view my salvation as complete when I arrived in Israel. I remember that when I took leave of my father – he was forced to remain in the ghetto, while I had received a deportation order to a labor camp – both he and I had absolutely no doubt that we would never meet again in this world. At that time, my father said to me, "I hope that you will get to the *Eretz Yisrael*." This was the supreme expression of hope for salvation.

When my mother suggested that I take a picture of the family with me, I refused. I told her that I had no need of such memories, that we would meet again. I could not allow myself to give expression to the feeling that I had no hope of ever seeing my parents alive again. Yet, I did not want to give my parents any hint that such thoughts resided within me. I took leave of my parents with a heavy heart and went to the labor camp. All that I took with me was a small Bible, Mishnah, and a booklet written by Rabbi Kook.

I admit to you today, that during those days I was very pessimistic. Many doubts gnawed at my heart. I only hoped I could die in *Eretz Yisrael*, even if I did not live there.

When the Russians liberated us from the labor camp, we no longer had any sense of reality. We had lost all contact with the world around us. I told my friends that I was going to Israel. They looked at me as if I had taken leave of my senses.

At the end of the war, I planned to go from Hungary to Bucharest, and from there to Israel. The caravan was planning to leave on the Sabbath. An argument began among us whether we were allowed to desecrate the Sabbath in order to join the caravan. I argued vigorously that to begin our journey was a matter of life and death, and thus it was permitted to desecrate the Sabbath. I could not help remembering that only a few weeks beforehand, a Russian soldier had placed a loaded gun next to my heart.

Certainly, these are sufficient reasons to offer combined thanksgiving to God for saving me and for allowing me to reach Israel. Yet there exists another more complicated, more profound reason for my insistence upon combining these two focal points in my life – salvation and my *aliyah* – into one personal holiday.

During the past forty years, I have often recalled the horrors that I lived through. Millions of Jews were murdered in the Holocaust – yet I was saved. Was I saved because God singled me out and made sure that I would not suffer the same fate as millions of others of our people? Or rather was it a mere case of chance? The verse states, "And I will surely hide My face on that day" (Deut. 31:18). When God hides His countenance from us, it is because, as the verse tells us, "And if you walk contrary to me... then will I also walk contrary to you" (Leviticus 26:21–24). Nahmanides explains that God, in effect, tells us, "I will leave you in the hands of chance" (Commentary on Job 36:7). Perhaps God had decided to leave His people in the hands of chance and, as a part of a fortunate accident, I was saved. If such is the case, then my salvation was a result of God acting in a contrary manner with His people, and not because He saw fit to single me out among millions!

If I positively knew that the Holy One, blessed be He, chose me, that God had singled me out for some special purpose, then such knowledge would, indeed, place a great burden upon me. I doubt that I would have been able to live up to and achieve what was expected of me. Yet, I would gladly relinquish all the wealth and riches of the world, if it were true that God had chosen to bestow His grace upon me, as an individual among millions.

These doubts plague me until this day. Clearly, the answer lies in the hands of God, and because I do not know the answer, I do not have the boldness to designate a specific day as a holiday because I was saved. Thus I combine both focal points of my life, my salvation and my *aliyah*, into one personal holiday. And yet, I still feel that heavy burden.

I am a simple person. Nevertheless, I sensed that I had to garner all the power within me, doubling and redoubling it, in order to recompense for those who are no longer with us. This knowledge gave me the daring and courage to accomplish things that were far beyond my normal abilities.

Whatever the case, this is certainly a year of thanksgiving and praise – and I intend to offer thanksgiving for salvation, and praise for *Eretz Yisrael*.

My association with *Eretz Yisrael* is one that was ingrained in me from early childhood. My family had been in the process of moving before the war came upon us. Even during my earliest years, *Eretz Yisrael* and the hope of the Messianic redemption were a very tangible and real part of my life.

Let me try to relate one of the most memorable occasions of my childhood. I must have been only four or five, but I still remember everything with total clarity. We were in *heder* (school) and playing in the yard. Suddenly, I saw a great ball of fire come out of the sky – I guess I must have been gifted with an active imagination. I told my friends what I had seen, and we decided that this was a sign that the Messiah was coming! The whole *heder* became very excited. What do children do when they expect the Messiah? We all ran together to the water tap in the yard and washed our hands in order to purify ourselves for the arrival of the Messiah! I can still remember the rush and the crowd at the water tap. There was an old, gnarled tree in the yard and we began to dance around it and sing.

I came from what was considered to be a modern home in those days; however, I was still able to absorb what was meant by waiting for the Messiah. A child's imagination knows no limits in regard to the Messiah!

We also had dreams as young boys – dreams of many things, and, above all, dreams of *Eretz Yisrael*. It was, and still is, difficult for me to understand how many people seem to be able to live without visions and remain bereft of dreams.

During the difficult days that followed – and the tribulations that I underwent were nothing compared with those Jews who found themselves in Auschwitz – I became very pessimistic, even though previously, I had always been optimistic. I suddenly found myself making peace with the reality that surrounded me. Perhaps my attitude was due to the influence of my teacher and rabbi, Rabbi Haim Yehudah Halevi, a great and holy man, who introduced us to the Lithuanian method of study. When the worst of moments came upon us, I asked him what would become of all our dreams. His response was immediate. He told me that the very core of all those dreams – their very essence – was to fulfill the will of Heaven. And if this – what we were undergoing – was the will of God, then we would achieve our dreams. It seemed that everything had become corrupt. I felt that we should begin to prepare ourselves to sanctify the Name of God (i.e., to die).

One of the most depressing periods was while I was in the labor camp. One day we were sent to the ghetto which had been emptied of all Jews. While there, I discovered a letter of my teacher and rabbi, full of his comments upon Chapter "*HaSholeach*" in Tractate *Gittin*, dispersed all over the floor. Among these papers I also found his rabbinical ordination, signed by Reb Chaim Ozer [Grodzinsky] and Reb Barukh Baer [Leibowitz]. I hoped in my heart that, perhaps, he was still alive somewhere, and I gave these papers to another student of his, but they disappeared.

We managed to take a small Torah scroll with us from the ghetto, and some other friends managed to smuggle out a small Talmud.

The month of Elul marked the last days before the retreat of the Germans. We managed to blow the *shofar* for Rosh HaShanah and to pray with a quorum, and we tried, as much as possible, to desist from work [that was forbidden by the Torah]. Every moment, every second that we could feel like Jews, was treasured and savored.

During one of those days, while we were reciting the *Selihot*, the order came for us to head towards the central part of the city. When we started to walk back, we realized that the whole army was in retreat, as the Russian Army had begun to advance. We took the Torah scroll with us. As the Russians continued to advance, the city began to empty. The soldier who was in charge of us left to try to find out what he should do with us. We tried to take advantage and escape, but after a few hours most of us were captured again. The soldier threatened to kill us, and even our offer of money and bribes no longer had any effect. When we came to a bridge, we suddenly heard the fire of a machine gun. It seemed to be nearing us and, to our good fortune, the soldier ran away in fear of his life.

That was the eve of Yom Kippur. We found ourselves in a ghost town. There was no other living thing left there. We came upon the Jewish communal center… the same house where I had once lived together with my parents…

We went to the basement and waited for Yom Kippur. With us was a Hassid who managed to find the *mikvah*, and we were able to immerse ourselves before Yom Kippur. We divided the bread that we had. Then we found a *mahzor*. One person read aloud from it and we all followed. That is how we prayed in a *minyan*.

Once again, the Germans got the upper hand and the Russians began to retreat. German guards moved through the city and we could hear shooting everywhere. When we arose on the day after Yom Kippur, we were very hungry. My cousin and I went to my parents' apartment and there we found some rotten bread, covered with green mold. The joy was unbelievable! We scraped off the mold, divided the bread between us, made the blessing and ate it.

Meanwhile, we heard someone crash through the gate downstairs. They were screaming for the Jews to leave the basement. My cousin and I went into one of the inner rooms in the apartment. We tried to decide whether to say Psalms (in hope of living) or *viddui* (confession, to prepare for death). I, the pessimist, decided to say *viddui*, while my cousin recited Psalms. In the end, both of us recited the *viddui* and Psalms. The German soldiers came to the apartment and went through each of the rooms, but they did not enter the room where we were hiding. It was a miracle!

In the hard days that followed for all Europe, from time to time we found ourselves with different groups of young people, who were trying to decide how to escape and over which border they should cross. Again, I must admit to you, that I was numbered among the pessimists. I claimed that there was no reason to escape, the Germans were searching for us; all that remained for us to do was to prepare ourselves to sanctify the Name of God.

When I finally did arrive in Israel, I met a former friend who had been with me during those times. He had already become a member of Kibbutz Kfar Etzion. When he saw me, with the hoe in his hands, he yelled in anger: "You! Yehudah! You were saved?! You, the one who told us to be ready to die in sanctification of God's Name?" He could not forget me, nor my former words. He was a hot-tempered man, and this was his first reaction to seeing me alive in Israel. When he calmed down, he finally asked me, "Yehudah, have you remained true to your beliefs? Are you still religious?"

I immediately answered him. "And if I did not remain religious? Then what? Would it then be easier to understand all that has taken place? Do things become simpler for one who has lost his faith?"

I clearly experienced the hand of God during the Holocaust – only I did not understand its meaning. It was so clear – so abnormal; so unnatural; so illogical. I was not in Auschwitz, but I saw the Jews who were being taken there. I saw regiments of Germans who were not going to the Russian front, but rather guarding the trainloads of Jews that were headed to the death camps. It was against all military logic and interests. Can one possibly begin to understand such madness? I saw the hand of God in everything. It was not natural; it was not human. I saw the hand of God, but I did not understand its significance. The establishment of the State of Israel does not explain why millions of Jews were led to their deaths. I do not accept the theory that has since been espoused by many, that the State of Israel gives reason and answer to the Holocaust.

There is one thing that I must emphasize. I never said the blessing, "Blessed art Thou, Lord our God, King of the Universe, who did not make me a gentile," with such fervor, as I used to recite it during those dark days. Specifically during those days, especially during those days – despite everything, I was proud to be counted among the murdered and not the murderers.

The Holocaust has become deeply ingrained within the consciousness of our people, even if we are not always aware of its influence upon us. I see the influence of the Holocaust in everything that has occurred since then: in the flight that many have taken from Judaism and in the return that many are embarking upon in search of their Jewish heritage and roots; in extremism; in Kahanism; and in Peace Now. I believe and hope that there is a possibility for inner change. The trials and tribulations of our people refine us, and even though many of our experiences seem to have a negative and adverse effect upon us, our nation is becoming better. The time will soon come when we will reveal the inner beauty of the entire nation of Israel.

We live during a very unusual and unique era, and we are not always aware of its nature. My beard has still not turned white with age, and yet during the course of my life I have seen, as our Sages have said, "a world built, destroyed, and rebuilt." I have seen Jews being led to Auschwitz; I have seen Jews dance at the establishment of the State of Israel; I have seen the great victories of the Six-Day

War; I have traveled with soldiers to the Suez Canal. I have lived through an epoch, in the shortest span of time. It is hard to believe that in such a short lifetime one could witness so many changes.

Today, the State of Israel stands at the focal point of world history. It is clear that we are living in a period of great change and, as such, it demands of us great deeds. It necessitates sacrifice; it hungers for creativity; it requires accomplishment; it compels us to take action.

From day to day, from year to year, changes take place. To live in such a period, to really and truly live it; to see and understand the dynamics and intensity of Jewish history as it unfolds before us; to gaze upon the great events – upon each one, in and of itself, and upon all of them combined – while we maintain the correct perspective, knowing that it is just a part of the whole; to sense the process of redemption as it unfolds before our very eyes; to know our responsibility in this world, at this time and in this place; to perceive what it is that God demands of us, here and now – all this creates a grave responsibility which one can neither escape nor ignore.

I am the man, poor in worthy deeds, who has seen communities in desolation, and who has merited to behold a land rebuilt.

> Sorrow and sighing, while I was upon a strange and foreign land; gladness and joy, when I came up to Jerusalem. (from the *Kinot*)
> Deliver my life from the sword... I will declare Thy name to my brethren; in the midst of the congregation I will praise Thee. (Psalms 22:21–23)
> For a small moment have I forsaken thee; but with great mercies will I gather thee. (Isaiah 54:7)

One thing remains clear:

> Upon Mount Zion there shall be deliverance. (Obadiah 1:17)

Confronting the Holocaust as a Religious and a Historical Phenomenon

By Rabbi Yehudah Amital[1]

"ON THE NINTH of Av, both the First and Second Temples were destroyed" (Mishnah *Ta'anit* 4:6). Indeed, our mourning for the burning of God's House stands at the center of the fast day of *Tishah be-Av*. Yet there is a tragedy worse than the destruction of the Temple. We read in Psalms (79:1–3):

> A psalm of Assaf: God, foreigners have come to Your inheritance; they have defiled Your holy sanctuary – they have made Jerusalem into ruins!
> They have given the corpses of Your servants as food for the birds of the heavens, the flesh of Your pious to the beasts of the land.
> They have spilled blood like water around Jerusalem; but no one buries.

---

1. Based on a discourse delivered in Yeshivat Har Etzion in July 1998; transcribed by Roni Goldenberg; translated by Yoseif Bloch; adapted by Rabbi Reuven Ziegler.

Concerning the heading of this psalm, the Sages comment (as cited by Rashi, *Kiddushin* 31b, s.v. *Istaya*):

> "A psalm of Assaf?" It should be "a dirge of Assaf!" Rather, interpret it thus: Assaf sang over the fact that God spent his fury on the sticks and stones of His House, and thereby He left a remnant of Israel; otherwise, there would not be a survivor left. Thus it says: "God has spent his fury, for he has ignited a fire in Zion" (Lamentations 4:11).

To add any explanation to this midrash would merely detract from it.

A short time ago, someone said to me, "I have gone through a great deal of Holocaust literature, and I now find it difficult to recite the *Kinot* of *Tishah be-Av* or to read the book of Lamentations. Everything described there pales in comparison to the Shoah!" I replied to him: "Is this a problem? On the contrary, this is exactly how *Tishah be-Av* should be. If one does not feel that Lamentations and the *Kinot* pale in comparison to the Shoah, the only explanation is that he is suppressing the memory of the Shoah."

To our great distress, we are witness today to the widespread suppression of the Holocaust from our religious consciousness. Admittedly, it is difficult to deal with the Shoah. One of the ways of dealing with it, which certain people have employed, is simply removing it from our minds, ignoring it – not in the historical sense, but in the religious and spiritual sense. I am not speaking of the pernicious phenomenon of Holocaust denial, which maintains that the Shoah never happened. Rather, I am referring to the absenting of the Shoah from the public memory and from our religious awareness, whether consciously or unconsciously – particularly here in Israel.

Belittling the Holocaust and the Degradation of Language

When people use loaded words like "Auschwitz," "Majdanek," "Nazis," etc., to describe other phenomena – serious though they may be – we find a belittling of the Shoah. Using terms derived from the Shoah to describe acts of terrorism will cause future generations to come to a point where only the historians among them will be able to differentiate between the Holocaust and Israel's wars. The carelessness of such speech is bound to bring us to a future where the term "Shoah" itself will come to be a general term for a disaster to the Jewish people, and perhaps "World War II" will be a synonym for the German destruction of our people.

When Jews use against Jews terms borrowed from the world of Holocaust images, they too belittle the Shoah. Whether it is left-ists calling Israeli soldiers "Judeo-Nazis," or rightists shouting "S.S." and "Gestapo" at police officers – both belittle the Shoah, even if the ultimate intent of their protests is good and their aim is for the sake of Heaven.

The Omission of the Shoah from our Religious Consciousness

A more serious phenomenon is the suppression of the Shoah from our religious consciousness. We stand silent before the enormity of the Shoah, and we have no answer. "And Your faithfulness in the nights" (Psalms 92:3) – even when it is darkest, we believe that God is faithful to us. This is one of the tests with which God tries us. Despite everything, we continue to cling to God, echoing the ironic lament: "We fled from You to You." But as for a reply, there is none.

Certain groups and certain rabbinical authorities presume to provide an explanation for every tragedy and disaster; they know how to answer, for example, why a certain number of children were killed in an accident. Many times, they attribute this to the sins of others. Let us imagine: if we asked one of those rabbis, "You have before you two scenarios: here a million and a half children were killed, and here ten; now explain this" – what would he say? "I have an answer for the ten, but none for the 1,500,000?" Hardly. Thus, the compulsion to provide an answer for the deaths of ten children compels us to remove the Shoah, a tragedy on a scale that we cannot begin to comprehend, from our collective religious memory – for one who has not done so can never claim, for any tragedy, "I have an answer!" I do not even speak of the educational implications of such an approach – if there is an "explanation" or a pat "answer" for everything, what will you tell your child when he or she asks: "Why did the Shoah happen?"

In the Religious Zionist camp as well, which sees the rebirth of the Jewish people in its land as part of a process of redemption, there are those who disregard the Shoah. The claims are familiar: "The redemption process began in the time of the aliya of the students of the Gaon of Vilna and continues to our day, like the morning star's light shines forth and grows ever brighter." They thus ignore, in pragmatic terms, the Shoah.

Is redemption expressed only by the blossoming of the Land of Israel and measured only by the extent of our control over it? And what about the Nation of Israel? Is what happens to the Jewish People not tied to the concept of redemption?

Such a destruction never happened before to the Nation of Israel. Can this destruction truly be made to fit into the redemption process? Seeing the redemption process as continuous and unwavering, constantly gaining strength and progressing, implies ignoring the Shoah.

In 1996, I was asked to participate in a panel discussion. At one point, one of the participants asked me: "Is it still possible to refer to the State of Israel as 'the dawn of our redemption' now, after four cities were given over to the Palestinians as part of the Oslo Accords?" Immediately, a rabbi, one of the leaders of the Religious Zionist camp, stood up and replied, "It is an *a fortiori* argument: if, seventy years ago, Rabbi Kook in his correspondence could refer to the embryonic State of Israel as 'the dawn of our redemption,' certainly we can, all the more so, do likewise today!"

Yet, in my mind, a question remained: "All the more so?" Is that really true? Was not our world destroyed in the intervening seventy years? Did the most terrifying event not happen in the meantime?

This approach, found among some members of the Religious

Zionist community, also ignores the Shoah, springing from a personal inability to deal with it. In the past, very grave opinions were expounded regarding the Holocaust: there were those who claimed that the Holocaust was a sort of price that the Jewish People had to pay in order that the Jewish State could be established. There are those who claimed that the State of Israel is the divine compensation for the destruction of the Holocaust. There were even those who claimed that the Shoah was the only way – or, at least in practical terms, became the impetus – to compel the Jews of Europe to immigrate to the Land of Israel. These are very difficult claims, approaches that I find hard to countenance at all. Moreover, these sorts of claims inspire a gut reaction, a natural aversion that causes me to worry less about them than about the historical and religious view that ignores the Shoah, disregards and omits it absolutely from our collective memory – which is infinitely more dangerous.

The Absence of the Shoah from Our Service of God

A third point that I wish to address relates to the basis for our divine worship at the present time.

In *Hovot Ha-levavot* (*The Duties of the Heart*), Rabbenu Bahya ibn Pekuda develops the notion that our service of God is based on gratitude to Him. "The Gate of Unity" and "The Gate of Distinction" precede "The Gate of Divine Service." In "The Gate of Distinction," Rabbeinu Bahya expands on the need to constantly think about God's kindness; the obligation of divine service thus springs from belief in His unity and recognition of His good. Rabbeinu Bahya addresses this at the opening of "The Gate of Divine Service" as well.

More than a few modern rabbis and preachers have continued to espouse the idea of gratitude as a basis for worshipping God. Such, for example, was Rabbi Dessler's approach, in the years preceding the Shoah.[2] The question is, understandably: after the awesome devastation of the Jewish People in the Holocaust, how – if

2. Dessler, *Strive*, vol. 1, pp. 153–5.

at all – can we still talk about our worship of God being based on gratitude or recognition of God's grace?

On my first Yom Kippur after being liberated from a Nazi labor camp, I prayed with other survivors in a cramped cellar. I cannot fully describe the storm of emotion that I felt then, but I will try to reconstruct some of that feeling.

I was young then. I had no children. My parents had been murdered along with most of the population of our town. Among the survivors in that small room, there were people who had lost their children, parents, spouses and siblings. They prayed, and I with them. Was their worship of God based on gratitude? Can a Jew who has lost his wife and children possibly serve God on the basis of recognition of His kindness? Can a Jew whose job was the removal of the charred remains of corpses from the crematoria of Auschwitz be capable of serving God on the basis of gratitude?

No, not in any way, shape, or form! But where, then, does that leave us?

"Even If He Kills Me, I Will Still Trust in Him!"

The Talmud records (*Yoma* 69b):

> Rabbi Yehoshua ben Levi says: Why were they called "The Men of the Great Assembly?" Because they returned the [Divine] crown to its ancient glory.
>
> Moshe came and referred to God as "The Great, Mighty, and Awesome God" (Deut. 10:17).
>
> Jeremiah came and said, "Foreigners are prancing in His sanctuary; where is His awesomeness?" – so he did not call Him "The Awesome" (Jeremiah 32:18).
>
> Daniel came and said, "Foreigners subjugate His children; where is His might?" – so he did not call Him "The Mighty" (Daniel 9:4).
>
> [The Men of the Great Assembly] came and said, "On the contrary! This is His might, that he subdues His inclination and shows patience to evildoers; this is

His awesomeness, for if God were not awesome, how could one nation [i.e. the Jews] survive in the midst of all the others?"

How then could [those prophets] have acted so and uprooted a Mosaic decree? Rabbi Elazar said: Since they knew that God is truthful, they would not lie to Him.

The parallel passage in the Yerushalmi (*Megilla* 3:7) cites an even more strongly-worded answer to the final question:

Rabbi Yitzchak bar Lazar said: These prophets knew that their God is truthful, therefore they would not [hypocritically] flatter Him.

The term used here is particularly harsh – "*chanufah*," which refers to insincere flattery designed to ingratiate oneself with someone more powerful. This behavior is abhorrent to God, as the *Korban ha-Edah* (ibid.) notes:

They told the truth, "for a flatterer will not be allowed to come before Him" (Job 13:16).

Divine service must be built on truth, not on falsehood or fawning flattery. Therefore, the prophets who felt that attributes such as "The Great," "The Mighty," or "The Awesome" could not in their times be used accurately to describe God, refrained from using such terms – despite the fact that they realized that they were deviating from the Torah's language and from the text that Moses had instituted.

This is true also of our issue. Within the era that saw the greatest destruction in the history of the Jewish People, it is impossible to base our divine worship on the foundation of "recognition of His good." Of course, we must always remain aware of God's daily acts of kindness, and must sincerely pray, "*Modim anachnu Lakh*" – "We thank You … for Your wonders and kindnesses at all times, evening, morning and afternoon." But while gratitude should certainly constitute one component of our divine service, it cannot serve as the entire foundation of our worship.

Rabbeinu Bahya, in the tenth section of his *Hovot ha-Levavot*, "The Gate of Love of God," sets out a different path of divine service:

> … One of the pious men would rise in the middle of night and declare: "My God, You have starved me, You have left me naked, You have set me to dwell in the gloom of night; and You have taught me Your strength and Your greatness. If You incinerate me in flame, I will continue only to love You and rejoice in You."
>
> It is as Job (13:15) said, "Even if He kills me, I will still trust in Him," and to this idea [Solomon] the wise man hinted when he said, "A bundle of myrrh (*tzeror ha-mor*) is my beloved to me, and he shall rest between my breasts" (Song of Songs 1:13). Our sages said, by way of derivation, "Though He constricts and embitters me (*meitzer li u-meimer li*), He will sleep between my breasts."

At the highest rung of religious development depicted in *Hovot ha-Levavot*, "The Gate of Love of God," Rabbeinu Bahya bases divine love not on gratitude but on faith, which persists even in an era of divine concealment.

The Mishnah (*Sotah* 5:5) states:

> On that very day, Rabbi Yehoshua ben Hyrcanus preached: Job served God solely out of love, as it says: "Even if He kills me, I will still trust in Him."

The Gemara (*Sotah* 31a) adds that it is only possible to explain the verse the way it is read, not according to the way it is written. Thus, the word "*lo*" in the verse "*Hen yikteleni, lo ayahel*" is to be spelled *lamed-vav*, yielding the translation above. It is impossible to interpret the verse as it is written, with the word "*lo*" spelled *lamed-alef*, yielding the translation, "If He kills me, I will no longer trust in Him."

This is also the explanation of the verse "Were Your Torah not my delight, I would have perished in my misery" (Psalms 119:92). The verse is not directed only to the "delight" of Torah study in particular, but rather to the whole concept of clinging to God (*devekut*). We do not know how to explain this *devekut*, but it is a bond that lies at the core of our very being.

In the wake of the Shoah, to whom can we still flee? To where can we flee? The answer is clear: "We have fled from You to You."

I have recounted the following story many times. Shortly after I arrived in *Eretz Yisrael*, I visited Kfar Etzion and chanced upon a friend whom I had known during those dark days. When he saw me, he cried out, "Yehudah – is it you? You were saved? You, who always preached to us that we have no hope and should prepare to die as martyrs sanctifying God's Name – you were saved!?" His next question was: "Did you remain religious?" I replied, "Had I not stayed religious, would all of the questions have been answered? Would the whole phenomenon then be understandable?"

I once had a conversation with Abba Kovner, may he rest in peace. He was a leader of the revolt in the Vilna Ghetto and an important Hebrew poet. I said to him, "I don't know whose test was greater, mine or yours. Your banner was faith in man. After the Shoah, can you still believe in man? I believe in God, Whom I cannot understand. But man should be fathomable – so what do you believe in now?"

The verse "Were Your Torah not my delight, I would have perished in my misery" has a broader meaning. *Knesset Yisrael* wonders, "How could I ever have persevered without God?" How can anyone survive without God? Without God, one simply could not cope with all the problems besetting him. It is not in spite of undergoing a test of this magnitude, but rather because of it, that we need our faith in order to survive.

"A bundle of myrrh is my beloved to me; he shall rest between my breasts" – although He constricts and embitters me, He shall rest between my breasts.[3]

3.   *Shabbat* 88b.

A Kaddish for the Martyrs
of the Holocaust

By Rabbi Yehudah Amital[1]

A GENERATION AGO, the Chief Rabbinate of Israel declared that the Fast of the Tenth of Tevet, which marks the beginning of the destruction of the Temple, would also be observed as a Holocaust Remembrance Day. Specifically, it would be the day to recite kaddish for relatives whose exact date of death we do not know. Just as the Tenth of Tevet thus has acquired a dual significance, so does the kaddish itself that we recite on this day.

On the one hand, kaddish is recited by each individual for his relatives. On the other hand, when many individuals recite kaddish, when the whole congregation recites kaddish, then it assumes additional meaning. To the extent that we explore this additional meaning of the communal kaddish, the kaddish of each individual will be elevated higher and higher, until the kaddish of each individual will itself attain a power and depth that never existed in the kaddish prayer as recited in past generations.

At the time of death of every individual Jew, the Holy One's

---

1. This discourse was delivered on 10 Tevet 5750 (January 7, 1990), and was translated by Kaeren Fish.

great Name is diminished, as it were, and so we add to it by reciting kaddish. This may be said of the kaddish of the individual.

But the communal kaddish is the innermost and most authentic expression of the Jewish nation. It demonstrates our faith's attitude towards everything that is bound up with the word "Holocaust" – a word that is only a code for all that took place there. Since there is no word or sentence or article or book that could describe what happened, we use this code word: Holocaust.

By reciting kaddish as a congregation, the Jewish nation expresses its feelings towards the Holy One in the wake of the Holocaust. Our religious attitude towards the Holocaust revolves around two axes, both of which find expression in our religious literature.

One axis is the fathomless cry and demand to Heaven: "My God, my God – why have You abandoned me?" (Psalms 22:2). "You would be in the right, O Lord, if I were to contend with You, yet nevertheless I will reason these points of justice with you: Why does the way of the wicked prosper? Why are the workers of treachery at ease?" (Jeremiah 12:1). "Your eyes are too pure to behold evil, nor can You look upon iniquity; why do You look upon those who deal treacherously, and hold Your peace when the wicked devours the man more righteous than he?" (Habbakuk 1:13).

The second axis is a position of subjugation towards God, as expressed in the words of Moses our Teacher: "The Rock Whose work is perfect, for all of His ways are justice" (Deut. 32:4).

On the one hand, there is the great question: Why have You hidden Your face from us, why have You forgotten and abandoned us? It is true that the ways of God are hidden, but You bless man with knowledge, You have given us intelligence, human understanding, and according to human understanding there is no justification for the murder of hundreds of thousands of young children who never tasted sin. No sin, however grievous, can justify to the human mind the burning of tens of thousands of mothers with nursing infants in their arms.

No worldly attainment can compensate for the murder of

those millions. All the claims about the establishment of the State of Israel serving as compensation for the Holocaust are hollow. Neither the State of Israel that exists in reality, that fights bloody wars for its existence from time to time, nor the ideal State of Israel, as in the vision of "Every man under his vine and under his fig tree" (Micah 4:4), can justify even partially what the nation of Israel went through during the Holocaust years. There is no honest religious response without this plea: "You would be in the right, O Lord, if I were to contend with You, yet nevertheless I will reason these points of justice with you."

On the other hand, the nation of Israel bows its head, declaring before God: "The Rock Whose work is perfect, for all His ways are justice… Righteous and upright is He" (Deut. 32:4). There is an irresolvable contradiction between these two positions. But that is the power of the nation of Israel – that despite the questions that have no answers, we justify God's judgment. This is the great test of the nation of Israel, the last test in the final stages of the exile and before the redemption: to understand nothing, and nevertheless to declare, "The Rock Whose work is perfect."

This is the inner significance of the communal kaddish, and this is also what gives significance to the kaddish of each individual. A kaddish such as that which we recite on Holocaust Remembrance Day has never been heard in such depth in all of Jewish history – a kaddish that expresses this great faith. "The Rock Whose work is perfect," together with "Your eyes are too pure to see evil." This is what gives the strength, the power, the depth to the kaddish of each individual.

One who was there – in the valley of killing – could not but see the hand of God; things were so unnatural, so unintelligible, so illogical. I saw thousands of evil Nazi soldiers standing, waiting, sitting and doing nothing, unable to reach the Russian front because of the trains that were crammed with Jews. How is it possible to understand that at the end of that great war, with the defeat of that terrible persecutor, may his name be blotted out, his last words were, "The Jews won!"

I shall not go into detail, but anyone who was there saw that the events were not natural. I saw the hand of God, but not the explanation, the meaning; He spoke to me – but I understood nothing. We saw the hand of God, we saw God's word, but what was He saying?

If there was a single point of light in the Holocaust, it was this: there were two camps there; on one side the camp of the murderers, and on the other side the camp of the murdered. Happy are we that we belonged to the camp of the murdered. The heavens and earth can testify on our behalf: if the nation of Israel had been given the opportunity to reverse roles, the nation of Israel would have said that it is preferable to be among the murdered than among the murderers. This is a historical point of light that cannot be overshadowed.

Facing a world of murderers, a world that stood by as the blood of millions was shed – we stood on the other side; all the world on one side and we on the other. We know, as Maimonides states in his *Epistle to Yemen*, that all the hatred that the nations of the world feel towards us is because of our Torah, because of our closeness to the Holy One, and therefore we say, "It is for Your sake that we are killed all day long, that we are regarded as sheep to be slaughtered" (Psalms 44:23). But at the same time we state before God: "If we forgot the Name of our God and spread forth our hands to a foreign god, would not God search this out? For He knows secrets of the heart" (ibid., 21–22).

It is not an easy test to maintain our faith after all that, and to say, "May God's great Name be exalted and sanctified." But my heart goes out to those Jews who have no faith, who say, "I believe in man," and that is what gives them strength. For we have seen how far man can degenerate; happy are we, how good is our portion, that we believe in the Holy One, Blessed be He, concerning Whom it is written, "My thoughts are not your thoughts" (Isaiah 55:8), even with all of our questions. But to say, "I believe in man," and to exist like that? My heart goes out to them.

Instead, we have to proclaim, "Be comforted, be comforted, My people, says your God. Speak tenderly to Jerusalem and declare to her that her term of service is complete, that her sin has been pardoned, for she has suffered from God's hand double for all her sins" (Isaiah 40:1–2). Her sin has been pardoned, she has suffered double for all her transgressions that were before, and those that have been since. We still lack psychologists of sufficient depth, of sufficient power, to examine what is happening to people today after the Holocaust. The nation of Israel attempts to suppress the memory the Holocaust, to repress it in every possible way, but who knows if the spiritual destruction that afflicts us does not flow from those scenes that the nation suppresses in its heart?

I have on prior occasions cited the Gemara's interpretation (*Shabbat* 88b) of the verse, "A bundle of myrrh (*tzeror ha-mor*) is my beloved to me" (Song of Songs 1:13) – although He constricts and embitters me (*meitzer u-meimer li*), "He shall rest between my breasts." This evening we express all that is in our hearts, all that we have to say before the Holy One, Blessed be He. Our assembling tonight in large numbers says something great about the nation of Israel. Despite our lack of comprehension, despite all our questions, we nonetheless declare: "*Yitgadal ve-yitkadash Shemeih rabba*," May God's great Name be elevated and sanctified.

Biographical Glossary

Akiva, Rabbi (c. 50–135 CE), was one of the leading *Tannaim*, laying the foundation for the Mishnah through his teachings. He enthusiastically supported Bar Kokhba's revolt, and died a martyr's death at the hands of the Romans.

Aviner, Rabbi Shlomo (1943–present), a disciple of Rabbi Zvi Yehudah Kook, is a leading Religious Zionist rabbi and a prolific author. He is Rosh Yeshivah of Ateret Kohanim in the Old City of Jerusalem and Rabbi of Beit El.

Bahya ibn Paquda, Rabbi (second half of the 11th century), was a religious judge in Saragossa, Spain, and is known particularly for his ethical work *Duties of the Heart*.

Dessler, Rabbi Eliyahu (1891–1954), of London and Bnei Brak, was a leading Mussar thinker, especially renowned for his work *Mikhtav Me-Eliyahu* (rendered into English as *Strive for Truth*).

Ben Koziba, Simon, known as "Bar Kokhba" (Aramaic for "Son of a Star"), was the leader of the last Jewish revolt against Rome in 132–135 CE.

Harlap, Rabbi Ya'akov Moshe (1883–1951), was a close disciple of

Rabbi A.Y. Kook and a rosh yeshivah of the Mercaz Harav yeshivah founded by Rabbi Kook.

Herzog, Rabbi Yitzhak Isaac (1889–1959), was the first Chief Rabbi of the State of Israel.

Kook, Rabbi Avraham Yitzhak ha-Kohen (1865–1935), was the first Chief Rabbi of Mandatory Palestine and founder of the Mercaz Harav Yeshivah. An original thinker and prolific author, he has had a lasting influence on the State of Israel and the Religious Zionist movement, in particular.

Kook, Rabbi Zvi Yehudah ha-Kohen (1891–1982), son of Rabbi Avraham Yitzhak ha-Kohen Kook and rosh yeshivah of the Mercaz Harav Yeshivah, was responsible for disseminating and interpreting his father's teachings and served as leader of and driving force behind Religious Zionism.

Kovner, Abba (1918–1987), was the leader of the partisan underground organization in the Vilna Ghetto during the Holocaust and later became an important Israeli poet and writer affiliated with the socialist Ha-Shomer Ha-Tza'ir movement.

Maimonides, Rabbi Moshe ben Maimon (1138–1204), preeminent medieval halakhic codifier and philosopher.

Nahmanides, Rabbi Moshe ben Nahman (1194–1270), leading Spanish talmudist, biblical exegete and kabbalist.

Reines, Rabbi Yitzhak Ya'akov (1839–1915), was one of the first rabbis to be active in the Zionist movement and an important visionary of Religious Zionism. He founded and headed the Mizrahi organization and headed a progressive yeshivah in Lida.

Glossary of Terms

ALIYAH: Immigration (lit., ascent) to the land of Israel.

AVODAT HASHEM: Service of God.

ERETZ YISRAEL: The land of Israel, promised by God to the Jewish people.

GEMARA: Rabbinic commentary expounding upon the simple legal code of the Mishnah; compiled approx. 500 CE.

HALAKHAH: The body of Jewish law, providing guidelines for all aspects of life.

HAREDI: Ultra-orthodox Jews, often associated with anti-Zionist or at least non-Zionist views.

HESDER: Five-year program in Israel that combines Torah study in a yeshivah with army service.

HESTER PANIM: The "hiding" of God's presence in the world.

HILLUL HASHEM: Desecration of God's name.

KIDDUSH HASHEM: Sanctification of God's name.

KINOT: Mournful poems or songs that are recited on Tishah be-Av (the ninth of the Jewish month of Av) to lament the destruction of the two Temples.

MISHNAH: Code of rabbinic law compiled approx. 200 CE.

MITZVAH: Divine commandment.

MUSSAR: Improvement of behavior through greater adherence to moral and ethical values; name of movement that emerged in Russia in the 1800s, led by Rabbi Israel Salanter.

ROSH YESHIVAH: Head of a yeshivah (see below).

SHOAH: the Holocaust.

SHULHAN ARUKH: Authoritative code of Jewish law, compiled by Rabbi Yosef Caro in the 16th Century.

TANNAIM: Rabbis who lived during the first two centuries CE whose teachings were codified in the Mishnah.

TISHAH BE-AV: the ninth of the Jewish month of Av, observed as a fast day in commemoration of the destruction of the first and second Temples.

YOM HA-ATZMA'UT: Israel's independence day, observed by many as a day of religious significance.

YESHIVAH: Institution of higher education devoted to Torah study.

Bibliographical Abbreviations of Works
by Rabbi Yehudah Amital

A Kaddish: "A Kaddish for the Martyrs of the Holocaust," *Ot Va-Ed – Pirkei Iyun U-Meida*, N.P. 1990; translated in this volume.

A World Built: "A World Built and Destroyed and Rebuilt: A Television Panel Discussion," *Yalkut Moreshet* 22, 1977 [Hebrew].

Commitment: "Commitment vs. 'Connecting' – The Current Crisis of our Youth," *Alei Etzion* 10, 2001, pp. 33–43; reprinted in his collection, *Between Religious Experience and Religious Commitment: Five Addresses on Youth in Crisis*, Alon Shevut 2003; archived at http://www.vbm-torah.org/archive/sichot61/12vayechi.htm.

Confronting the Holocaust: "Confronting the Holocaust and a Religious and a Historical Phenomenon," originally in *Alon Shevut Bogrim* 13, 1999, pp. 45–54; translated in this volume.

Cry of an Infant: "To Hear the Cry of an Infant," *Alon Shevut Bogrim* 1, 1994, [Hebrew].

Da'at Torah: "What is the Torah Source for *Da'at Torah*?" *Alon Shevut Bogrim* 12, 1997 [Hebrew].

Darkness:	"When I Sit in Darkness, God is My Light," *Alon Shevut* 96, 1982 [Hebrew].
Eight Princes:	*Eight Princes of Men: In Memory of the Eight Students of Yeshivat Har Etzion who Fell in the Yom Kippur War,* Alon Shevut, 1975 [Hebrew].
Ethical Foundations:	"The Ethical Foundations of Rav Kook's Nationalist Views: On the Significance of Rav Kook's Teaching for our Generation," originally published in *The World of Rav Kook's Teachings,* eds. B. Ish-Shalom and S. Rosenberg, New York 1991; revised and corrected English translation in *Alei Etzion* 2 (1995), pp. 13–27. References are to the latter edition. Corrected translation is archived at http://www.vbm-torah.org/archive/rya2-eth.htm.
Facing the Challenge:	"Facing the Challenge of a New Reality," *Nekudah* 17, 1992, and *Alon Shevut Bogrim* 1, 1994 [Hebrew].
Forty Years Later:	"Forty Years Later: A Personal Recollection," *Alon Shevut Bogrim* 3, 1994, pp. 85–90 [Hebrew]; translated in this volume.
Guardian of Israel:	"Guardian of Israel, Guard the State of Israel," *Alon Shevut Bogrim* 9 1996 [Hebrew].
HaMa'alot MiMa'amakim:	*HaMa'alot MiMa'amakim* [The Steps from the Depths], Jerusalem and Alon Shevut 1974 [Hebrew].
Letter:	"Letter," *Alon Shevut* 100, 1982, pp. 55–62 [Hebrew].

Minorities: "The Torah's Attitude Towards Minorities in the State of Israel," *Daf Kesher* vol. 2, Alon Shevut 1990, pp. 340–343; also printed in *Judaism and Democracy: Lectures at a Day of Study*, Jerusalem 1989; archived at http://www.etzion.org.il/dk/1to899/200daf.htm [Hebrew].

Nation Before Land: "The Nation of Israel Before the Land of Israel," *Sevivot* 22, 1988 [Hebrew].

Not By Their Sword: "Not By Their Sword Shall They Inherit the Land… For You Have Desired Them," *Daf Kesher* vol. 2, Alon Shevut 1990, pp. 46–48; http://www.etzion.org.il/dk/1to899/131daf.htm [Hebrew].

Not Everything: "Not Everything is *Halakhah*," *Alon Shevut Bogrim* 13, 1999; also in *Meimad* 15, 1998 [Hebrew].

Obligations of Conscience: "Matters of Obligation and Obligations of Conscience," *Daf Kesher* vol. 1, Alon Shevut 1988, pp. 28–30; http://www.etzion.org.il/dk/1to899/010daf.htm [Hebrew].

Political: "A Political or an Educational Message?" *Alon Shevut* 100, 1982, pp. 34–54 [Hebrew].

Religious Significance: "The Religious Significance of the State of Israel," *Alon Shevut* 151, 1998; also *Alon Shevut Bogrim* 11, 1998 [Hebrew]; translation appears at http://www.vbm-torah.org/yyerush/atz59.htm.

Secular Jews: "A Torah Perspective on the Status of Secular Jews Today," *Alei Etzion* 2 (1995), pp. 29–45. This article appeared earlier in *Tradition* 1988, and can be found at: http://www.vbm-torah.org/archive/rya3-chi.htm.

Sing to Him: "Sing to Him, Praise Him, Speak of All
His Wonders," *Alon Shevut Bogrim* 9, 1996
[Hebrew]; translation appears at http://www.
vbm-torah.org/yyerush/atz57.htm.

Social Challenges: "The Social Challenges Confronting the State
of Israel," *Alei Etzion* 10, 2000, pp. 9–18; archived at http://www.vbm-torah.org/archive/
ryasoc1.htm.

This is the Day: "This is the Day that God has Made; Let Us
Be Happy and Rejoice in It," *Alon Shevut* 94,
1982; also in *Shedemot* 100, 1987 [Hebrew].

Understand the   "Understand the Years of Each Generation,"
Years: *Alon Shevut Bogrim* 13, 1999 [Hebrew].

Bibliographical Abbreviations of Works
by Other Authors

Abreviation	Author	Title
Aviner, Holocaust	Aviner, Rabbi Shlomo	"Holocaust and Redemption: The Significance of the Holocaust in Light of Our Faith" in *Faith in the Holocaust: A Collection of Lectures*, Jerusalem 1980, pp. 51–52 [Hebrew].
Aviner, *Lavi*	Aviner, Rabbi Shlomo	*A Nation Like a Lion* (*Am ke-Lavi*), vol. 2, Jerusalem 1983 [Hebrew].
Aviner, Realism	Aviner, Rabbi Shlomo	"Messianic Realism," *Morasha* 9, 1975 [Hebrew].
Aviner, *Waves*	Aviner, Rabbi Shlomo	*Your Waves and Billows Passed Over Me*, Jerusalem 1990 [Hebrew].
Bat-Yehudah	Bat-Yehudah, Geulah	*The Man of Lights: Rabbi Isaac Jacob Reines*, Jerusalem 1985 [Hebrew].

Abreviation	Author	Title
Brown	Brown, Benjamin	"Crossroads with No Way Out," *Akdamot* 2, 1997, pp. 85–99 [Hebrew].
Dessler, *Strive*	Dessler, Rabbi Eliyahu E.	*Strive for Truth!* (translation of *Mikhtav me-Eliyahu*), transl. Aryeh Carmell, 6 vols., Jerusalem 1985–1999.
Eliach	Eliach, Yaffa	"The Holocaust: A Response to Catastrophe Within a Traditional Jewish Framework," in *The Historiography of the Holocaust Period*, Jerusalem 1988, pp. 719–735.
Fackenheim, Faith	Fackenheim, Emil	"Jewish Faith and the Holocaust – A Fragment," *Commentary*, August 1968, pp. 30–36; revised version in Fackenheim, *Quest for Past and Future*, Bloomington 1968 (chapter 1). Citations here are from the original version.
Fackenheim, *Presence*	Fackenheim, Emil	*God's Presence in History*, New York 1972.
Filber	Filber, Rabbi Ya'akov	*The Morning Star (Ayelet ha-Shahar)*, Jerusalem 1975 [Hebrew].
Gorni	Gorni, Yosef	*Between Auschwitz and Jerusalem*, London and Portland, 2003.

Abreviation	Author	Title
Hutner	Hutner, Rabbi Yitzhak	"Holocaust – A Study of the Term, and the Epoch it is Meant to Describe." *The Jewish Observer*, Vol. XII, No. 8, October 1977.
Ish-Shalom	Ish-Shalom, Benjamin	*Rabbi Avraham Itzhak HaCohen Kook: Between Rationalism and Mysticism*, Albany 1993.
Kook, RAYH, *Letters*	Kook, Rabbi Avraham Yitzhak	*Letters*, 3 vols., Jerusalem 1962–5 [Hebrew].
Kook, RAYH, *Orot*	Kook, Rabbi Avraham Yitzhak	*Orot*, trans. Bezalel Naor, Northvale, NJ 1993.
Kook, RAYH, *Orot Yisrael*	Kook, Rabbi Avraham Yitzhak	*"Orot Yisrael,"* in *Orot*, Jerusalem 1976 [Hebrew].
Kook, RZYH, *Discourses*	Kook, Rabbi Zvi Yehudah	*Discourses of Rabbi Zvi Yehudah*, ed. Rabbi S. Aviner, Keshet n.d. [Hebrew].
Luz	Luz, Ehud	*Wrestling with an Angel: Power, Morality and Jewish Identity*, New Haven 2003.
Michman, Connection	Michman, Dan	"Was There a Connection Between the Holocaust and the Establishment of the State?" in D. Michman and Y. Weitz, *In the Days of Holocaust and Destruction*, unit 12 (At the End of the Holocaust), Tel Aviv 1992 [Hebrew].

Abreviation	Author	Title
Michman, Faith	Michman, Dan	"And You Have Afflicted Me With Faith – Trends in Faith During the Holocaust," *Milet* 1, Tel Aviv 1983 [Hebrew].
Nehorai	Nehorai, Meir Zvi	"Rav Reines and Rav Kook: Two Approaches to Zionism" in B. Ish-Shalom and S. Rosenberg (eds.), *The World of Rav Kook's Thought*, New York 1991, pp. 255–267.
Piekarz	Piekarz, Mendel	"Hassidism of Poland Between the Two Wars and in the Edicts of 5700–5705," *The Holocaust*, Jerusalem 1990 [Hebrew].
Ravitzky, Fate	Ravitzky, Aviezer	"Fate and Free Choice: Messianism, Zionism and the Future of Israel in the Divided Religious Views in Israel" in A. Har-Even (ed.) *Israel Facing the 21st Century*, Jerusalem 1984 [Hebrew].
Ravitzky, Freedom	Ravitzky, Aviezer	*Freedom upon the Tablets*, Tel Aviv 1999, [Hebrew].
Ravitzky, Messianism	Ravitzky, Aviezer	*Messianism, Zionism, and Jewish Religious Radicalism*, Chicago 1996.
Schwartz, Challenge	Schwartz, Dov	*Challenge and Crisis in the Rabbi Kook Circle*, Tel Aviv 2001 [Hebrew].

Abreviation	Author	Title
Schwartz, *Faith*	Schwartz, Dov	*Faith at a Crossroads*, Tel Aviv 1996 [Hebrew]
Schwartz, *Land*	Schwartz, Dov	*Land of Reality and Imagination*, Tel Aviv 1997 [Hebrew].
Schwartz, *Religious Zionism*	Schwartz, Dov	*Religious Zionism – Between Logic and Messianism*, Tel Aviv 1999 [Hebrew].
Schweid, Orthodox	Schweid, Eliezer	"Orthodox Religion Addresses the Holocaust", *Mahanayim* 8, 1995, pp. 10–35 [Hebrew].
Schweid, *Wrestling*	Schweid, Eliezer	*Wrestling until Day-break: Searching for Meaning in Thinking on the Holocaust*, Lanham 1994.
Statman & Sagi, Dependence	Statman, Daniel, and Sagi, Avi	"The Dependence of Morality on Religion in Jewish Thought," in *Between Religion and Morality*, eds. A. Sagi and D. Statman, Ramat Gan 1993, pp, 115–144 [Hebrew].
Statman & Sagi, *Religion*	Statman, Daniel, and Sagi, Avi	*Religion and Morality*, Amsterdam 1995.
Tau	Tau, Rabbi Zvi	Faith for Our Times: Paths in Understanding the Era, II, Jerusalem 1995 [Hebrew].
Urbach	Urbach, Ephraim	The Sages, *Cambridge MA 1975.*
Yerushalmi	Yerushalmi, Yosef Hayim	*Zakhor: Jewish History and Jewish Memory*, Seattle 1982.

Subject Index

Rabbi Amital's escape from, 133
approaching Land of Israel, 59
classifying Jews, 114
coming to power, 67
literature of thinkers who lived
    under, 8
as loaded term, 142
prevented from reaching front,
    128, 153
retreat of, 137
searching for Jews, 138, 139
Non-Jews,
    apostate killed by, 114
    distinction of Jews from, 71,
        92–95, 111, 154
    loss of faith in, 92
    relating to their homelands, 125
    treatment of, 92–95, 98, 101–102,
        106, 110

O

Orot, 31n33, 65, 67, 101
Oslo Accords, vii, 59n106, 64, 144

P

Peace Now, 139

R

Radak, 10–11
Ravitsky, Aviezer, 23–25, 27, 69–70
Rashi, 125, 142
Redemption,
    See also Beginning of
        redemption, Zionism
    Rabbi Amital's hope for, 135–6
    current process of, 140, 144
    Holocaust as preparation for, 71
    of Israel, 140, 144
    Jews longing for, 97

of the Second Temple as model,
    120–121
universal, 78, 106
war as part of, 31
Refugees, 79–80, 83.
    See also Survivor(s)
Reines, Rabbi Yitzhak Ya'akov, 158
    See also Salvation, simple
    Rabbi Amital following the
        example of, 78–79
    on revelation of God in history,
        26n19
Religious Zionists/Religious Zionist
Camp,
    Rabbi Amital as a leader of, 6, 9,
        21, 36
    ascribing religious and messianic
        significance to State of Israel,
        vi, 43, 56–57, 62, 64, 69, 144
    dependence on Halakhah of,
        104, 123
    dependence on Nahmanides of,
        18, 104
    disregarding the Holocaust, 42,
        144–145
    divergence of Rabbi Amital
        from, viii, 7, 60–66, 103–106
    and Divine immanence, 50, 69
    involvement in modernity, 104,
        117, 123
    on Jewish sovereignty and the
        Messiah, vi
    on morality within Halakhah,
        101–103
    neglect of morality/moral
        degradation of, 103–106, 123
    openness to secular education
        and culture, 25, 104, 123
    reliance on human action, 60–61

Source Index

BIBLE		
Genesis	18:19	122
	32:24	94n14
	32:25	93
	44:20	15
Exodus	24:7	126
Leviticus	10:3	51
	19:2	124
	26:21–24	11–12, 47n80, 134
Numbers	14:15–16	86n176
	23:9	94
Deuteronomy	4:32	117
	6:18	124
	10:17	146
	29:3–4	52, 133
	31:18	11, 47n80, 134
	32:4	53–54, 152–153
	32:7	23

MAIMONIDES, MISHNEH TORAH		
Laws of the Foundations of Torah	5:10	107n62
Laws of Repentence	2:10	95, 97n29
Laws of Fast Days	5:3	117n3, 120n9
Laws of Prohibited Sexual Relations	19:17	95
	12:24	95n20
Laws of Gifts to the Poor	10:2	95n20
Laws of Slaves	9:8	96n21
Laws of Kings	1:3	117n3, 120n9

About the Author

M OSHE MAYA was educated at Yeshivat Ha-Negev, Yeshivat
Sha'alvim and Bar Ilan University, and is currently complet-
ing a doctorate in Jewish History at Haifa University. He resides in
Mitzpe Hoshaya in the Galilee and teaches at the Ulpanit in Tiberias
and at Yeshivat Ha-Kibbutz Ha-Dati in Ma'aleh Gilboa.